TALKING ABOUT DEATH

talking
about
death

A DIALOGUE
BETWEEN
PARENT AND CHILD

Earl A. Grollman

A new edition with a Parent's Guide
and recommended resources

Illustrated by Gisela Héau

Beacon Press

Boston

Text copyright © 1970, 1976 by Earl A. Grollman

Illustrations and calligraphy © 1970 by Gisela Héau

Beacon Press books are published under the auspices
of the Unitarian Universalist Association

Published simultaneously in hardcover and paperback editions

Printed in the United States of America

(hardcover)   9   8   7   6   5   4   3   2   1

(paperback)   9   8   7   6   5   4   3   2

Library of Congress Cataloging in Publication Data

Grollman, Earl A
   Talking about death (rev. ed.)
   Bibliography: p.
   SUMMARY: A read-along picture book explaining death to young
children with an extensive guide for parents. Includes list of
pertinent organizations, books, tapes, and films.
    1. Children and death.   2. Death— Juvenile literature.
[1. Death]   I. Héau, Gisela.   II. Title.
BF723.D3G717   1976   155.9′37   75-37786
ISBN 0–8070–2372–8
ISBN 0–8070–2373–6 (pbk.)

To my mother, Chana Resel,
who taught me about life

CONTENTS

TO PARENTS

"Mommy, what does dead mean?" "Why did grandfather die?" "Where did he go?" "Will I die, too?"

One of the most difficult problems for parents is helping a child through the crisis of death. Youngsters' feelings and perspectives are too often overlooked— an understandable situation in our often death-denying, death-defying culture. The word D-E-A-D has become the new four letter word of pornography. Most modern parents are convinced that they should be honest in discussing the biological processes of birth. But when it comes to life's end, they may fall strangely silent.

A recent study disclosed that most parents cannot recall how they told their children about the death of someone loved. The period surrounding the event was a complete blur. Adults struggling with their own grief did not believe a child would understand the tragic situation. A youngster's denial, silence, or sense of shock was taken to mean the child could not possibly know that death had occurred and therefore was not in mourning.

On the contrary. A child growing up today is more aware of the reality of death than you may realize. Grief is a deeply human emotion, as normal as playing, laughing, crying, sleeping. Grief is a way of saying, "I miss you" or, "I'm so sorry for all the things I've said and done." When you avoid children's reactions, you magnify their fears and replace reality with fantasy and psychological defenses.

This book is written with the hope that when a death does occur, your child may be sympathetically guided towards an understanding of its real meaning. For the most effective results you should first carefully read the contents of section 2, *A Parents' Guide for Explaining Death to Your Child*. Determine in advance the best method of interpreting the material: what points to emphasize, what lessons to be underscored. Those with religious convictions will supplement the discussion by sharing spiritual resources. In this dialogue, it is the grandfather who has died. The reader can easily substitute another name or relationship.

Children have too long been terrified by secrecy and adults' private and furtive misery. When you read the book aloud, you may suddenly discover that you share the same emotions as those of the youngsters you're attempting to counsel. As Emerson observed in his journal, "Sorrow makes us all children again." The challenging task is to realize that death is as certain as the rain and separation as final as yesterday. Just as death is inevitable, so is life.

Earl A. Grollman

INTRODUCTION

Solomon Grundy,
Born on Monday,
Christened on Tuesday,
Married on Wednesday,
Took ill on Thursday,
Worse on Friday,
Died on Saturday,
Buried on Sunday,
And this is the end of
Solomon Grundy.

How many children have recited this simple nursery rhyme about life's beginning and ending? Youngsters are confronted with the fact of death in word and song as well as in the natural world of plants, animals, family, and friends. The question is not whether children should receive death education, but whether the death education they are receiving is helpful and reliable. Understanding is a life-long process that continues from childhood through old age. Death education begins when life begins.

How to Read This Book

Among the many ways of dealing with death, the one most surely doomed to failure is your attempt to ignore it. You must tell your children immediately about a death in the family. They should not hear the news from an acquaintance. Delay makes it all the more likely that they will be told by the wrong person in the wrong way.

Approach the discussion gently and lovingly; the tone of your voice—warm, sympathetic, kind. *What* is said is significant, but *how* you say it will have a greater bearing on whether your youngsters develop unnecessary fears or will be able to accept, within their capacity, the reality of death.

Before you read this book to the children, make sure that the house is relatively quiet, that there is ample time to be alone with them. It is neither necessary nor desirable to read the book in one sitting. Most youngsters could not possibly absorb the information at once in a helpful way. Proceed gradually, according to their intellectual and emotional capabilities.

Pause from time to time to let them express what they feel, and ask what they wish to know. Allow them to reveal their innermost fantasies and fears. "Will Grandfather someday come back to life?" "Am I a sissy if I cry?" "Is death a kind of terrible punishment?" "Are you angry that he died without saying goodbye to you?" And on the brighter side, "What are some of your happy memories of the good times you spent together?" Children need to talk, not just be talked to. Respect their individual responses, for in the long run they must find their own answers to the problems of life and death.

Permit them to vent the emotions of grief: anger, tears, guilt, despair, and protest are natural reactions to family disorganization. They may cry at nothing and laugh at everything. They may express hostility as well as affection. Grieving in any form is a necessary healing process.

You may be asked to repeat an explanation. Even an adult who first experiences a terrible crisis often says, "I don't believe it, It's a nightmare. It can't be true." So gently say it again. Denial is their way of coping with and working through a difficult situation.

On the other hand, a parent need not offer more information than the child is really seeking. A satisfactory response to the question "What is death?" should not be an involved theological explanation but a simple, factual reply, "A person does not breathe. The body is still, quiet, peaceful." Too many parents project their own unresolved problems upon children. If you are in doubt, simply ask, "Just what is it you want to know?" Over-answering reflects your own anxiety. A complicated answer brings confusion and distraction.

Children often mistake the meanings of words and phrases. I was once asked by a young girl, "How long is death?" I responded, "Death is permanent." The youngster said, "Oh, then it's not so bad." Noticing my bewilderment she said simply, "My mother has permanents all the time. It lasts for about six months."

Children may ask questions to test their parents. Before answering, adults should understand the progression of thought leading to the inquiry. Otherwise, their reply could be misleading. When a boy was told that his grandfather died because he was old and sick, the child became preoccupied with his parents' health. He would cry whenever his mother and father had a simple cold. He discovered convenient reasons to stay away from nursery school and remain at home. "How do you feel?" he would ask again and again. The parents were irritated, not understanding their son was convinced that their own death might soon occur. To the child, the parents were old (an old person is someone fifteen years older than you) as well as sick. What the boy wanted to hear was, "I have a slight case of the flu, but I will get better."

be honest

Never tell your children what they will need to unlearn later. Avoid fairy tales and half-truths. Imaginative fancy only gets in the way when they are already having enough trouble separating the real from the make-believe. Youngsters need direct, simple, and honest information about death as about everything else. They need continuing reassurance and understanding.

There are no simple, foolproof answers to the mystery of death. Not only children but also adults differ more widely in their reactions to death than in their reactions to any other human phenomenon. There is no magic procedure that will comfort all people, either at the time of death or during the period that follows. Grief and adjustment do not work on strict timetables. While one person will pick up the threads of life and work out new patterns relatively quickly, another will find, even after a longer period, little discernible movement toward a meaningful future.

we're all diff.

After you have absorbed the *Parents' Guide*, read the section titled *For Further Help* describing additional resources for you and your children. Finally, the section *For Further Reading, Listening, Viewing* lists books, cassettes, and films which will help you to understand and talk about death.

When you die, you're dead.
Try saying that word, DEAD.
It is a hard word to say, isn't it?
Not hard to pronounce, really,
but hard to make yourself say.
Maybe because it's a sad word...
even a little frightening.
Let's say it again:
DEAD.
Now, let's say another word:
DIE.
That's what happened to grandfather.
Grandfather died.
He is dead.

It is not like playing cowboys and Indians.
"Bang! I shot you. You are dead!"
And then you start all over again
and play another game.

DEAD IS DEAD.
It is not a game. It is very real.
Grandfather is gone.
He will never come back.

When something goes wrong,
        we may pretend
    it didn't happen.
We hope it isn't true.
        When grandfather died,
we didn't want to believe it:
" Maybe the doctor was wrong."
" Maybe grandfather just went away
on a long trip and will come back."
    But we know that we are only
            fooling ourselves.
    Grandfather is dead.
        We miss him.
        We love him.
But we cannot bring him back to life.

What is dead ?

Remember when you saw a dog
that was hit by a car ?

He was lying on the road
still . . .

not breathing . . .

not moving . . .

His heart was not beating .

He would never breathe or
move again .

HE WAS DEAD .

It is the same for people .

The body does not move .

It does not breathe .

The heart does not beat .

The body is still . . .

quiet and peaceful .

There is no hurt, no pain, no life .

Like plants.

You put seeds in the ground.
They grow.
They bud.
And beautiful flowers appear.

After a time, the flowers fade.
They fall off.
They die.

For flowers, and for all of us –
For everything, "there is a season."

Which means, there is a time
for every living thing to
grow and to flourish
and then to die.

When a flower dies,
it is dead.
Life has left it.
That flower will never grow again.

We can remember how
beautiful it was,
but now it is gone.
"To everything
there is a season."

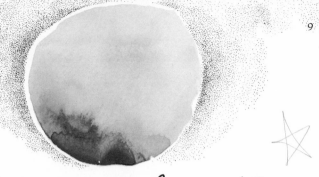

These words come from the Bible.
"To everything there is a season
and a time to every purpose —
A time to be born, a time to die;
A time to cry and a time to laugh."
          These words tell us that
Just as there is joy in life,
               there is also pain.
Just as there is happiness,
               there are also tears.
We understand life by both
the light and the darkness.
What do you think this means?

Death is very sad.

We miss grandfather.
We want him, NOW.
We miss him so much that we
may even cry.
What is wrong with that?
Nothing. It's all right.

It is one of our ways of showing how
much we miss and want him.

Are you worried?
Afraid you did something wrong
and that's why grandfather is not here---
as a punishment to you?
OF COURSE NOT!

Grandfather did not die because you may
have been bad.
You did nothing to make him die.
Let me say it again.
You DID NOTHING TO MAKE HIM DIE!

Nothing you did had anything
to do with his death.
In fact you helped to make
him happy when he was with you.

But maybe you remember
times you were mean to him.
You may have said terrible words.

But all people are like that sometimes.
We may want to be good and loving,
but we do not always do the right thing.
Sometimes you may not have done the right thing.
Perhaps you made him unhappy.
But grandfather always understood.
He could forgive you.
HE LOVED YOU.
You had nothing to do with his death.

All people die.

Are you angry that grandfather died?

How could he do this to you?
How could he leave you?
Didn't he love you enough
to stay alive?
You feel left alone and lonely.
A little hurt, maybe.
Is that how you feel?

Let's talk about it.

Do you want to tell me
            some of the things
that are troubling you?
    Talking about them might help.
            I will listen.
    I will try to understand.
Because I, too, am trying to
            find some answers.
I, too, am troubled and sad.
        Did you know that?

Are you surprised that I
don't know all the answers
about death?

Don't be.

Even though no one really understands it,
death is something we must accept.
We can talk about it.
You can learn something from me.
I can learn something from you.

We can help each other.

We do know that
when grandfather died
there was a funeral.
Friends and family came together.
We went to Services.

We listened to beautiful prayers.
Everyone talked about grandfather
and his life.
We felt happy that people knew
grandfather was such a good man.
But we felt sad, too.
We cried.
We would never see him again.

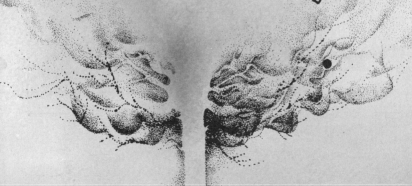

Then we went to the cemetery.
Remember, you asked about the place
that looked something like a big park.
But it was
filled with large stones,
one near the other.
That is called a cemetery.
On one of the stones
grandfather's name will now be written.
Grandfather's body is under the warm earth,
below the stone.
We will go together someday
to the cemetery.
For that is where grandfather's body is.

Of course, we shall have grandfather in

other ways.

But these ways are in our minds,

in our memories.

We know that we cannot see him

or talk to him.

But we can talk about him

and remember him.

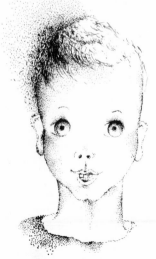

Tell me what you remember most about him.
Do you remember some
          of the funny things he did?
     Do you remember the times
you made him so happy?

Now he is dead.
But we remember him.
We can never forget that he died.
But we will always remember
that he lived.

A Parent's Guide to
Talking About Death

A PARENT'S GUIDE FOR

EXPLAINING DEATH

TO YOUR CHILD

PAGE 2

When you die, you're dead.

Can children actually understand death?

Parents have said, "Children under ten are too young to understand. Why burden them with concepts they cannot possibly grasp? Why not spare them adult thoughts and grief?" But death is around your children all the time. Even at a very young age they are confronted with that inevitable moment when life no longer exists: a pet is killed; a funeral procession passes by; a leader is assassinated; a grandfather dies. And they see pictures of people being killed in vivid color on television.

What should you tell your children about the words DIE and DEAD? The answers are related to the developmental age of your youngsters, the nature of the death, and their emotional involvement with it. Children of the same age differ widely in behavior and development: some are responsible and stable; others are immature and seem younger in relation to their years. Parents realize how different their own children are, even identical twins.

Do not try to precisely fit your youngster's perception of death into a fixed age category. For you as well as for your child the meaning of death is constantly reexamined as life changes. A concept of death undergoes a continuous process of maturation. The following are but general guidelines.

Stage One: Preschool Age

Psychologist Maria Nagy researched one of the first and most comprehensive studies of 378 children's perceptions of death. Her investigation demonstrated three recurring questions in a youngster's mind: "What is death?" "What makes people die?" "What happens to people when they die; where do they go?"

A preschool child may not believe that death is final. Death is like sleep: you are asleep, then you awaken again. Or taking a journey: you are gone, then you come back. A child experiences some aspects of what he or she considers "death" when Father goes to work or Mother to the supermarket. It is like playing "peek-a-boo" (from the Old English meaning "alive or dead"). One moment you are here, then you are not. Death is reversible.

Children may attribute life and consciousness to a dead person. The deceased continues to live in the confines of the casket where he breathes, eats, moves, goes to the toilet, and understands what is occurring in the world outside. A youngster may feel sorry because life in the grave seems so dull and drab.

Since death is perceived as a temporary phenomenon, the child may not comprehend sadness around him. After all, "If Grandpa is still breathing in the ground, won't he come back to us again?" Death and life are interchangeable. The child is further confused when he sees a dead bird lying on the ground and then views an identical kind of bird flying overhead.

"Death is final," parents assert positively. But how can it be so? The child hears older siblings tell ghost stories in which spirits of the dead continue to live. A minister's discussion of an afterlife suggests a return to life. The youngster watches a rerun of a television program in which an actor reported dead by a news commentator is still very much alive.

What do "final" and "forever" mean to a child who has little abstract sense of time or distance? What is important to the youngster is now, this very moment. "Tomorrow," "final," "forever" seem too far away to be concerned about. In living for the immediate, children are not concerned with their own death, especially if they are lucky enough to avoid accidents.

To a child death is usually thought of as accidental. One dies when run over by a car or attacked by robbers. Death may be associated with violence, particularly dismemberment. Death is not inevitable—people may live forever if they are fortunate and careful.

Stage Two: Ages five to nine

In mid-childhood youngsters are better able to understand the meaning of physical death because of their developing life experiences. For some there is a strong tendency to consider death as a physical manifestation in the form of a person or spirit. One religious child conceived of an angel of death with a long beard and fancy wings. Those who watched horror shows believed death was a boogeyman, a skeleton, or a ghost in white that made the rounds late at night.

At this stage youngsters often neither deny death nor accept its inevitability. A compromise is made. Death is "real" but only to others, namely, the aged. As Nagy says: "Death is still outside and is also not general."

Stage Three: Ages nine, ten, and thereafter

Children now formulate realistic concepts based on biological observation. Death is not a person but a perceptible end of bodily life. A dog runs into the street and is hit by a car. The animal can no longer get up to play. Dead is dead. It is very final and universal. It is brought about by natural as well as accidental causes. Death is that inevitable experience which happens to all including the child. (It is necessary to point out that many adolescents and even adults have childlike views of death. They "know" death is final, but their daily attitudes and actions are more consistent with the conviction that personal death is an unfounded rumor.)

Try saying that word, DEAD. It is a hard word to say, isn't it?

A young mother was extremely careful not to mention the word DEAD *to her three-year-old son. "I just want to protect him for as long as possible." When his grandfather died, she said, "We lost Grandpa today." The youngster replied simply, "So, let's go find him."*

People don't die anymore. They "pass on," "pass away," "perish," "expire," "go away," "are lost," or "depart." Euphemisms get in the way of children's understanding just as they are attempting to distinguish reality from a world of fantasy.

Often when you resort to euphemisms, you are only deceiving yourselves, not your youngsters. Children respond to your mood of sadness and pain. In a study entitled "Who's Afraid of Death on the Leukemia Ward?" Dr. Joel Vernick describes a concerted effort by the staff to conceal the diagnosis from children. All the hush-hush attempts were in vain. Even the very young realized in some way that they were seriously ill and could die at any time. Parents everywhere will testify that it is almost impossible to deceive children.

Avoidance creates further anxiety. Ignorance about death can be terrifying and disruptive. The most awesome reality is better than uncertainty. I have seen people, told that they had an incurable disease, breathe a sigh of relief and say, "I'm still frightened, but I know now what is really wrong with me." When you confront death, you begin to cope with the actualities of life. No one should be kept in emotional or intellectual isolation.

Evasion indicates your own inability to deal honestly with real situations. It encourages youngsters to "forget about things." Your children are human beings, worthy of respect and openness, not pretense and equivocation. Two of their greatest needs are for trust and truth.

DEAD IS DEAD·

Word was received of the death of a beloved grand-father. When the parents and two older brothers began to cry, the sister did, too. Then she began to laugh. Indignantly, the brothers demanded that she explain her strange behavior. "Well, Grandpa is coming back, isn't he? Why be sad?"

In some of their games children shoot each other "dead." Then they start all over again and play another game. In the world of fantasy, youngsters pretend that a crisis never occurred. Or that they have a magical power to make the deceased come back to life. After all, fairy tales have happy endings. Good people are rewarded and live happily ever after. Cinderella marries a prince; the wicked queen is compelled to dance in red-hot slippers until she dies.

The young attribute life to inanimate objects such as toys and playthings. One boy placed a marble in the sand and watered it with the conviction that it would grow. Children should under-stand that there is a difference between stuffed animals and real pets, between dolls and live babies, between man-made objects and living things. Puppets are broken; people die. Of all the manifold works of creation only the human being is able to know that he cannot live forever. An essential part of our human-ness is that we find meanings for death as well as for life.

Children must learn that certain things in life cannot be changed; all of us must live with the given. "Death is real. Grand-father is dead. He will never come back."

we didn't want to believe it.

*When President Kennedy's son John-John returned
on a visit to the White House following the death of his
father and saw his father's secretary, he looked up at
her and asked, "When is my daddy coming back?"*

Denial is a natural reaction to loss and takes many forms. In
a state of shock the survivor says, "No, not me. It's just a terrible
dream." One discusses the deceased in the present rather than
the past tense. The room of the loved one is left intact in antici-
pation of return.

Denial is encouraged by silence and secrecy. Adults insulate
a child with the hope of protecting themselves as well as their
youngster from the pain of loss. In James Agee's novel *A Death
in the Family* the child, Rufus, senses the parent's unwillingness
to discuss what occurred:

> When you want to know more about it (and her eyes
> become still more vibrant) just ask me, just ask me and I'll
> tell you because you ought to know. "How did he get
> hurt," Rufus wanted to ask, but he knew by her eyes that
> she did not mean at all what she said, not now anyway, not
> this minute, he need not ask; and now he did not want to
> ask because he too was afraid; he nodded to let her know
> he understood her.

I was once called to a home where a girl's father had just died.
When the daughter returned home, she was told the sad news.
Casually she said, "Oh, he died," Then a pause: "Is it all right
if I go out and play?" I considered the child to be insensitive and
thought, "Didn't she really love her father?" It was not until
later that I realized that the impact of death does not immediately penetrate the minds and the hearts of survivors. For example,
the most difficult time for a widow is not at the time of death
nor during the period of post-death activities such as the funeral
when she is surrounded by people sharing her sorrow. It is
days, weeks, months, and perhaps even a year later when she
realizes the full impact of her husband's death—of being alone.
Death is then very real.

A child may look unaffected because he is trying to defend himself against the death by pretending it has not really happened. The parent may be relieved: "Isn't it lucky! I am sure he misses his father, but he does not seem to be really bothered by it." A lack of response often signifies that the child has found the loss too great to accept and pretends secretly that the deceased is still alive.

The fact that you and your children at times go through moments of denial need not indicate an abnormal mourning reaction. When you are absorbed in some project, your pain is momentarily forgotten. Then like a sudden storm, anguish floods in. "My God, I'm talking about a church rummage sale and my husband just died!" Temporary forgetfulness enables a person to put aside the morbid, upsetting, and depressing aspects of death by refocusing upon the more constructive issues of the business of living.

" Maybe grandfather just went away on a long trip and will come back."

The young father was perplexed. His own father had just died and he did not know how to break the news to his four-year-old daughter. He finally said, "Grandpa is not feeling well. He went away for a long rest to California and will be there a long time." He hoped the little girl would not be too upset. The memory of the grandfather would gradually fade away and the youngster would accept his absence as being normal.

Instead the girl became angry. Far from being comforted and holding the memory of her grandfather dear, she reacted with deep resentment and asked, "Why didn't he say goodbye?" Adults' reactions are similar—death is a kind of desertion. A widow thinks, "How could he do this to me? Why did he leave me all alone?" Her euphemism for death is "when my husband left me," as if it were a willful act.

A youngster could develop a delusion that someday his grandfather will return. After all, he had been on vacations before and always came back. Or he could unconsciously assume, "Grandpa doesn't really care about me. He won't even write. Maybe I did something wrong and he is staying away to punish me." Then the problem of deception is further compounded: "Why is everyone so sad? The last time he went on vacation everybody was happy."

To say to a child, "Your grandfather went away on a long journey" is a way of providing temporary solace and easing the strain of Grandfather's absence. But, as stated earlier, there is no point in saying something false that youngsters must later unlearn. You are catering to misconception and fantasy. According to Freud, to many small children, death means little more than departure; disappearance is represented in dreams by going away on a journey.

There is no need to avoid the word DIE, especially since death is dramatized so frequently on television. A child will more readily understand a direct statement about death than some evasive term like "going away," which may lead to a fear that living people who go away may never return.

Why not simply say, "Grandfather died because he was sick"?

The grandfather died of a coronary after a long illness. The elderly man had been in and out of the hospital for years. It seemed natural for the parents to explain, "Grandpa died because he was sick."

People do become sick and die, but almost everyone who becomes ill survives. Youngsters often equate death with physical ailments and hospitals. They think, "Will I die when I have the flu, mumps, measles? What will happen when I go to the hospital to have my tonsils taken out?" You must make a distinction between a very serious illness and a simpler one.

A child may be terrified that he will die of some sickness that "took" his loved one. "I feel like Grandpa. My heart hurts me." The youngster becomes preoccupied with the physical symptoms that terminated the other's life; in a process of identification he transfers the symptoms to himself. It is necessary to repeat again and again, "Even though you and the person who died are in the same family, you are different individuals. I can truthfully tell you that you are in good health. You should live for many, many years."

What about using the word "heaven" to describe Grandfather's new abode?

We can't be selfish," the father said, seeking to ease the pain of his son, "God was lonely and wanted Grandpa with Him in heaven."

A concept of heaven may be difficult for a child to grasp. "But Daddy, if Grandpa is going to heaven, then why are they putting him in the ground?" Some children peer from an airplane window seeking the deceased loved one. Others hope rain coming down from heaven will bring Grandfather back to earth.

You may feel that your own beliefs are too stark for a youngster—that it would be more comforting to express a religious conviction you do not personally believe. So you spin out a tale of heavenly happiness while hopeless finality fills your own heart. You comfort the child by saying, "Grandpa will always be with us," while you mourn that person as irretrievably gone. Children have built-in radar and quickly detect your inconsistency and deception. Share honest religious convictions, but be prepared for further questions concerning simplistic theological terms.

... or, "God took Grandpa because he was so good. God wanted Grandfather for himself"?

"Isn't it beautiful! God chose Grandfather to be an angel because Grandpa was so wonderful and marvelous. God picks only the prettiest of flowers."

Despite the best intentions, a questionable religious approach is introduced. *You* may understand that the "Lord giveth and taketh away" in the sense that God who makes life possible also makes death necessary. But to assert that God wants the loved one "because the person was so good, the "prettiest flower," denies the truth that *all* individuals die—the good and the bad.

A little girl said, "I need and want Grandpa, too." She developed deep resentment against a God who capriciously robbed her of someone she loved. To state "God took him" or "God wanted him" could make God appear an enemy—vengefully striking one down for being virtuous.

Some interpret a young person's death in a similar way. "God loves the young and pure." Nonsense. There is no relationship between longevity and goodness. The righteous may die young but could also live to a ripe old age. One girl became so upset that she cried, "But I'm young and God loves me, too. Maybe I'll be the next one He will take away." To her God became a vindictive policeman, not a loving Father. Do not paint too beautiful a picture of the world-to-come. Some young children have attempted suicide in the hope of joining the absent loved one. By taking their own lives they intended to correct the loss and at the same time be with God in Paradise. Suffering and death should not be linked with either sin and punishment or reward.

37

Is it helpful to compare death with being asleep?

"The dog is so old and sick. See how slowly and painfully he moves. He shakes all over. Maybe the best thing is to put him to sleep."

It is natural to draw a parallel between "sleep" and "death." Homer in the *Iliad* alludes to sleep (Hypnos) and death (Thanatos) as twin brothers. Religious prayers often link the two words. Some pious people arise each morning and thank God for restoring them to life.

Be careful, however, to explain the difference between the two words; otherwise, you run the risk of causing a pathological dread of bedtime. Some youngsters toss about in fear of falling asleep, never to wake up again. They struggle with all their might to remain awake, terror-stricken that they will have Grandfather's kind of "sleep."

A familiar nursery prayer which has alarmed some children throughout the ages reads:

> Now I lay me down to sleep.
> I pray the Lord my soul to keep.
> If I should die before I wake,
> I pray the Lord my soul to take.

One little girl was convinced that God "killed" people during nightly sleep. An enlightened writer revised the bedtime prayer without anxiety-ridden overtones:

> Now I lay me down to sleep.
> I pray the Lord, Thy child to keep,
> Thy love guard me through the night,
> And wake me with the morning light.

Linking death with sleep could bring both misunderstanding and denial. After all, "if Grandpa is sleeping, won't he wake up?" Some funeral directors have contributed to the avoidance of death by calling a room in the funeral home a "slumber room."

The time has come when you must no longer respond to children with fiction and half-truths. Grandpa did not go on a long journey. He is not asleep. Loss is real; separation is painful; and death does indeed bring an end to life.

What is dead ?

"I know that I should discuss death with my children. But I'll be honest with you, I am confused myself. How would I begin?"

Do not begin by asking, "Have you ever thought what you will do when I die?" Such an introduction is too security-shaking for both parent and child. Nor should an initial explanation be based on dogma, belief, or theology. Philosophical interpretations are too abstract for a small child to comprehend.

Death and its meaning should be approached gently, indirectly, tenderly. An explanation might involve flowers and how long they last. Let your youngster watch those miniatures in nature with so many diverse forms, shapes, and colors, such as bugs, snails, butterflies. Once they moved, now are quietly still. Start with nonthreatening examples and proceed slowly, step by step, in accord with the child's ability to understand.

Remember when you saw a dog that was hit by a car?

"Why are you crying so hard? It's only a dog. It's not as if something happened to your parents. We can always buy another pet."

When a pet dies, your children are face to face with the real implications of death—its finality, the grief it brings. Your youngsters and the pet played together so often and now the fun is ended. Life is over.

Children may mourn more deeply for a pet than for a human being. There is more irony than humor in the story of a mother who said, "David, I don't know how to say this. Your doggie died." David did not seem too disturbed, so the mother thought her son had not heard her. She repeated her statement. David then became visibly shaken. "Oh, my God, don't tell me . . . I can't believe it. Tell me it isn't true. It's not so, is it?" The mother answered, "But I told you before and you acted so well. Why are you taking it so hard now?" David replied, "I didn't know my *doggie* died—I thought you said *Daddy* died."

The burial of a pet gives children an opportunity to act out their feelings and fears. A small boy's dog was killed by an automobile. His first reaction was one of shock and dismay, followed by outrage against his parents. He felt they were guilty because they had not taken proper care of the pet. (The boy behaved like an adult who rages against God for neglecting His charges.) Yet anger against the parents was a substitute for his own guilt, for the youngster had on occasion wished to be rid of "that awful pest." The child insisted that one of his favorite toys be buried with the dog. The toy served as a kind of peace offering to the offended pet. Now the lad was freed of anxiety and could continue to function effectively in his everyday activities. Ritual combined the dynamics of guilt, assuagement, and reparation—similar to the mourning behavior of adults. If a classroom pet dies a teacher might suggest that the children plan and carry out some kind of burial.

Do not rush out too quickly to find a substitute for a dead animal. Let your children understand that the pet cannot be exactly duplicated. Another collie may be purchased, but it will be different from the original one. Animals are not identical any more than human beings are. Wait a while for the youngsters to mourn their loss. If you get another pet, you might purchase a pet with different markings— and give the new animal a different name. Do not rob your child of the right to grieve, to cope with, and to master pain.

Like plants.

"Look in the woods. See those plants that are dying. Most of them will be dead before long. But look there. Other shoots are beginning to come up. Nature constantly renews itself. It's the same for people. Living and dying are part of human unfolding. Four billion of us are here on the planet Earth. Someday we will be no more. All things have a life-span—our bodies, trees, flowers, animals, and plants. Yet there will be other people, trees, flowers, plants to inhabit the world. Biologists tell us that everything that is alive is the renewal of something that died, cell for cell. These are the cyclic rhythms of nature—night and day, phases of the moon, seasons, lives of insects, seeds, plants, animals, people."

Children understand the mystery of death through an exploration of nature—its diversity and its sameness, its dependability and its unpredictability, its beauty and its grotesqueness. Water has various forms: rain, snow, ice, hail, lakes, oceans, streams, geysers, glaciers, and waterfalls. There are changes and growth each day of larva to butterfly and egg to tadpole and frog. New leaves replace old ones that die.

That which lives bequeaths seeds so that life may continue. Learning that death is part of life begins with the physical parting of the infant from the mother. While separation is sad and painful, it is an essential part of life and nature. What would happen to our crowded world if old people did not die as more babies are born? "There is a time for every living thing to grow and to flourish and then to die" (Ecclesiastes III:1).

" To everything there is a season..."
We understand life by both
the light and the darkness.

When her husband was at sea, a sailor's wife clothed herself in her finest garments. When the neighbors questioned her, she replied: "My husband's plans may change or perhaps a favorable wind will bring him home earlier; I want to make sure that whenever he arrives I shall be at my best."

In talking about death and darkness, you begin to value life and light all the more. A realization that there is "a time to die" adds a vital dimension and seriousness to living. An awareness of the winds of change—your final boundaries of existence— make it more urgent to be at your best, to really live.

Darkness makes light more precious; death makes the value of life more imperative—not in the sense of being morbidly pre-occupied with thoughts of dying, but in living life. The problem is not the allotment of a short life, but an extravagance in spending it. The personal tragedy lies in what you might do with your brief existence but do not—the love you do not give, the efforts you do not make, the powers you do not use, the happiness you do not earn, the kindnesses you neglect to bestow, the gratitude you have not expressed, the noble thoughts and deeds that could be yours if only you did not live as if you had eternity at your disposal. This is the dimension of holiness in time, doing your best to make *this* day more meaningful.

"It's too late," you may say, "I still have a part of my life ahead but I can't change those things in the past I should have done for my beloved. I didn't show real appreciation and affection. Now he is dead." In a sigh is found an insight; in sorrow, a jolt out of complacency. Make the memory of the deceased live! As darkness eventually changes into light, so you may convert adversity into good.

A story is told by a famous rabbi:

A king once owned a large, beautiful, pure diamond of
which he was justifiably proud. It had no equal anywhere.
One day the diamond sustained a deep scratch. The king
called in the most skilled diamond cutters and offered them
a great reward if they could remove the imperfection from
the treasured jewel. None could repair the blemish. The
king was sorely distressed. After some time, a gifted lapi-
dary came to the king and promised to make the rare
diamond even more beautiful than it had been before the
mishap. The king was impressed by his confidence and
entrusted his precious stone to his care. The man kept his
word. With superb artistry he engraved a lovely rosebud
around the imperfection and he used the scratch to make
the stem.

One can emulate the craftsman. When life bruises and wounds,
you can use even the scratches to etch a portrait of beauty,
memory, and love.

> I shall pass through this world but once,
> Any good, therefore, that I can do
> Or any kindness that I can show,
> To any human being
> Let me do it now. Let me
> Not defer it or neglect it, for
> I shall not pass this way again.
> —Steven Grellet

Death is very sad.

"My daughter really surprised me when her grand-mother died. She is such a tiny child, but she seemed more upset than most of the adults."

Grief is an expression of love. Mourning is an appropriate emotion for people of all ages. Children are no strangers to unhappy feelings—they know what it means to be mad, sad, guilty, afraid, lonely.

According to Dr. John Bowlby of London's Tavistock Clinic, children may experience three phases of a normal grieving process. The first is protest, when they cannot quite believe that the person is dead and they attempt, sometimes angrily, to regain him or her. The next is pain, despair, and disorganization, when youngsters begin to accept the fact that the loved one *is* gone. Finally, there is hope, when they reorganize their life without the deceased.

Children's responses to grief fluctuate according to their concepts of death, their developmental level, and the way they had related to the person now dead. Some will not speak about the individual who died; others will speak of nothing else. Some will cry hysterically; others will remain outwardly impassive and emotionless; while others may even laugh. Some will praise the deceased as the most wonderful person in the whole wide world; others will hate the individual for leaving them alone and abandoned. Some will blame themselves for the death; others will project their grief upon God, the physician, the clergy, the funeral director, or members of the family. Children's despair is often interrupted by a carefree mood, vacillating between sadness and playful joy. In short, reactions are varied and contradictory, often unpredictable.

Children should not be deprived of the right to grieve. They should no more be excluded from sharing grief and sorrow than they should be prevented from demonstrating joy and happiness. Each person should be given the opportunity to lament the end of life and love in his or her own way.

45

We miss him so much that we may even cry. What is wrong with that? Nothing. It's all right.

"Show me what a big boy you are. Be brave. Don't cry."

But crying is a natural emotion. A newborn enters life crying for more oxygen. In early life, tears are an infant's means of expressing needs, pains, and discomforts. Even after children are able to verbalize their desires, they continue to weep in order to release painful emotion.

Tears are a tender tribute of yearning affection for those who have died but are not forgotten. Weeping helps to assuage heartache—to express that inevitable depth of despair that follows the slow realization that the death is not a bad dream.

Do not be afraid of causing tears; they are like a safety valve. So often people deliberately turn a conversation away from the deceased. They are apprehensive of weeping that may follow. They do not understand that expressing grief is normal and helpful.

Children should never be discouraged from crying. Why should they be forbidden from expressing their inner feelings? They loved the person who died. They miss the individual. And they too need to relieve painful emotions.

Only the insensitive would say of a child who has experienced tragedy and remained dispassionate, "The youngster is taking it so well. He never cries." The old bromide, "Be brave!" encourages the child to bottle up true feelings and minimize loss. The youngster who stoically represses grief may later find release in an explosion more dangerous to his inner makeup.

Do not feel as if you have failed when you weep in front of your child. The opposite is true, for it expresses the undeniable fact that you too are human and need emotional release. It is better to say, "I could cry, too," rather than, "there, there, you mustn't cry." Some of the most tender experiences I have witnessed are parents and children weeping together and sharing the real meaning of the pain of separation.

A story drawn from the Bible that I often recount: "When Adam and Eve were banished from the Garden of Eden, God had great compassion and resolved to help them. However, the decree of expulsion could not be revoked. Man and woman would still have to be banished with grave affliction. God then considered a way to dignify and elevate their life of hardship. When the two primal beings left Paradise behind them for the last time, God created and bestowed His final gift—the gift of tears."

In our culture the gift of tears seems to be reserved for one sex: crying is mistakenly considered a female trait. This lesson is first demonstrated when a little fellow falls off a swing, bumps his head, and out of fright and hurt begins to cry. The mother or father quickly runs out of the house, picks him up, and says, "Quiet now, little man; big boys don't cry."

All people should be permitted to cry, fathers included. Some social scientists believe that the failure of men to outwardly express feelings may be one reason why they are more vulnerable to certain illnesses. From a physiological view, when there is emotional stress, gastric secretion increases. Crying not only helps relieve tension but aids in the excretion of lysozyme, which reduces the concentration of gastric juices. A result is a lower incidence of duodenal ulcers in females (six to eight times less frequent than in males.) Many believe that the lower incidence of accomplished suicides for women, as well as their longevity, may be attributed in some degree to their greater "freedom" to cry out feelings. You do not need statistics or clinical cases to demonstrate a truth known to many of us: whatever your age or sex, you simply feel better after a good cry.

While you will not deny a youngster the opportunity to weep, neither should you urge the child to display unfelt feelings. Youngsters should not be subjected to emotional blackmail in which they are urged to behave in some particular manner, such as remaining still when they need to run and jump. Each child reacts differently. Some children need to cry freely. Others may be able to get by with a few tears. There are some who may not weep at all for a grandfather who lived far away and did not touch the child's life. Youngsters feel confused and hypocritical when told to express a sentiment they do not honestly feel. There are other outlets for emotion besides tears. Allow them to express those feelings appropriate to their needs.

as a punishment to you ...
Grandfather did not die because you may
have been bad.

"You keep your bedroom like a pigsty. You will be the death of me yet." The mother died shortly thereafter. The boy suffered terrible guilt because he believed his sloppiness was the cause of her death.

There is a degree of guilt involved in almost every death. It is human to blame yourself for past failures. Adults who do everything in their power to make a loved one happy may search for ways they should have done more. After the Cocoanut Grove nightclub fire in Boston, one woman could not stop condemning herself for having quarreled with her husband just before his untimely death. Recrimination is an attempt to turn back the clock, undo the wrong things for which the survivor now feels guilty, and somehow magically to prevent the loss.

Guilt takes many forms. It can be directed outward with aggressiveness and hostility. "Daddy, why didn't you call the ambulance in time? If you had, Mommy would be alive today!" By projecting guilt upon someone else, the youngster is now blameless. Guilt may be turned inward causing depression. The child is unable to concentrate on schoolwork. He is too preoccupied with a sense of failure to join others in play. Some cannot sleep, and when they do, have recurrent nightmares. Others regress into bed-wetting and thumb-sucking. Unresolved grief is found in withdrawal, delinquency, excessive excitability, self-pity, and defiance.

More than adults, children are apt to feel guilt. In their experiences, bad things happen when they are naughty. If your son gets good grades in school, he is rewarded. On the other hand, when he hits his sister, he may be punished by losing television privileges. The "desertion" of a loved one must therefore be a retribution for wrongdoing. He searches his mind for the "bad thing" for which he is being penalized. Adults experience the same process. Everyone in the clergy has heard the question: "Why am I being punished?"

From a commonsense point of view, the youngster's guilt may seem unreasonable to the parents. Pangs of guilt are still agonizing, even when induced by a misconception of reality. One girl was told that in order to live she must eat. Since she did not eat her cereal the morning her father died, she concluded that she must be responsible for his death.

Parents inadvertently create guilt by unexplained or fictional interpretations. A college student reminisced about returning home from school when he was a first-grader to learn that his older sister "had gone away and would not come back." "Where did she go? What happened?" he inquired. "Don't ask so many questions," was the only response. For years he suffered recriminations, convinced in his own mind that he must have done something terrible to cause her disappearance. His guilt was only relieved when he took a course on "dying, death, and bereavement" at the university.

Young people believe in the power of magic, that, in the words of an old song, "wishing makes it so." When a girl contemplated a friend, thinking in anger, "How I hate him—I wish he would die" and the friend died, she felt accountable for the death.

Words too have their effect. "Why did I call him those terrible names? What will happen to me? Will God punish me?"

The living may feel guilty simply because they are alive. Perhaps they consider themselves censured for having wished that a sick person would hurry up and die. One thinks or says about the terminally ill, "It's enough. He is suffering so much. Why can't he go quickly and peacefully?" Then after death, one may be guilt-stricken for having wished that the afflicted individual could die with dignity.

Let children understand that nothing they said, did, or thought had anything to do with the death. You might say, "Perhaps you made him unhappy. He understood. He would forgive you. He loved you. You had nothing to do with his death. All people die."

Are you angry that grandfather died?

"Why did Grandpa do this to me? He always played with me on Sundays. Now he went away and left me. I hate him."

From denial, "No, not me," children turn in anger and say, "Why me?" The bereaved are often bitter and resentful for their misfortune; they may become irritable and difficult to manage.

"Bad Grandpa—he went away from me." The youngster recalls the occasional times his parents left him when they went on vacation. He was outraged. When they came home, he turned on them, saying, "Where were you? Why did you leave me?" Anger brought results. Not only did they return, but they brought him gifts. If irritation gets him what he wants, then his anger may bring back his grandfather.

The two expressions of anger—angry thoughts and angry feelings—are used to remove frustration. A first impulse of an enraged individual is to strike the people who cause the suffering. It is natural to wish to retaliate against those who have hurt you. You may understand this need to vent your own hostility, yet often you won't tolerate the behavior in your children.

Do not react to your children's anger with threats of further punishment. They have had enough guilt and pain. Instead, approach them with patience and respect. Listen as they tell you about their fears and animosity. If you say, "How dare you speak about your poor, dead grandfather that way," you bring the dialogue to a speedy conclusion, unsatisfactorily.

You might say, "We all have memories, both good and bad." Never scold them for feelings, or make them feel ashamed of their emotions, or tell them that they should only have good thoughts about the person who has died. If you and your child cannot recall unhappy memories of the deceased, then you may not yet have accepted the reality of the death.

I, too, am trying to find some answers. I, too, am troubled and sad. Did you know that?

"When my husband died, I didn't want my children to see me moping around the house. You just don't go around crying in front of your own kids."

As a member of the clergy I thought I too had to keep a "stiff upper lip." My role was to comfort others. I thought, "How would it look if I displayed weakness?"

I believed this for many years. I did not understand that what I had mistakenly labeled "weakness" was really being human. Since I have been in the same congregation for more than a quarter of a century, I have developed strong emotional bonds with many members. No longer do I attempt to stoically repress all my feelings. On occasion I weep with the people I am con-soling—for I, too, loved the deceased. My display of emotion has not diminished the survivors' esteem. To the contrary, on more than one occasion I heard the remark, "If the rabbi can shed a tear, then why is it so wrong for me?" If it is therapeutic for people to grieve for a loss, should professionals be exempt? Physicians, nurses, social workers, clergy, funeral directors— please take note: your honestly felt emotions should be expressed.

When you mourn, you give your children a model to follow. They then understand that it is acceptable for emotion to be out in the open. If you do not grieve, they may invent reasons for your lack of feeling: "Mommy isn't even crying. She never did love Daddy." Or, "Mommy is so jumpy lately. She must be angry at me for something I did."

It is helpful to call an emotion by its rightful name. "I am ANGRY . . . SAD . . . HURT." To avoid it does not make it go away. Denial drives suffering inward where it could emerge later in a disguised or undesirable reaction. Don't you really feel better when your thoughts are expressed? "Did you know that I too am troubled?" Grief is worked through when child and parent understand and reveal their uncomfortable feelings.

PAGE 16

*Are you surprised that I
don't know all the answers
about death ?
Don't be.*

---

*"My children look up to me and respect me. God
forbid that I should let them down and tell them that I
too am confused over their grandfather's death."*

You do not diminish yourself in your children's estimation
when you tell them you don't have complete answers. They
probably reached this conclusion a long time ago. If not, they
must someday realize the truth: adults are not all-powerful and
all-knowing. You demonstrate your maturity when you display
honest uncertainty. It is far healthier for you and your children
to seek understanding together rather than to attempt to protect
your parental authority with glib half-truths or evasions.

Don't be didactic; leave the door open. You might help the
child struggle with the problem by saying, "People the world
over have different approaches to that question which has no
final answer. Everyday we learn more about life's secrets. Tell
me what you think. I want to know. Maybe you would like to
hear about some of my thoughts and experiences." An open,
frank discussion encourages further mutual probings.

Your children will both challenge and help you. In your quest
to find answers for them, you may discover more explanations
for yourself. Their direct, honest, and often embarrassing doubts
may compel you to come to terms with your own thoughts and
feelings.

A wise person once said, "I have some good answers. Do you
understand the real questions?" Not all questions have final
answers. Unanswered problems are part of life.

53

We do know that
when grandfather died
there was a funeral.

"*Of course, our children shouldn't go to the funeral. They're much too young.*"

A most important aspect of maturity is the ability to say good-bye. We live in a period of rapid change where people continually move in and out of our lives. From the time we are born we are taught to say hello. Seldom, if ever, do we learn to say goodbye. Since many have not learned the importance of leave-taking, we carry an unfinished business in our life's relationships.

The funeral is a rite of separation . . . the bad dream is real. The presence of the casket actualizes the parting experience, transforming the process of denial to an acceptance of reality. It is an opportunity to say goodbye. The deceased will no longer be part of the familiar environment.

Yes, the funeral may be sad. But sadness is an integral part of the life cycle. Mental health is not the denial of tragedy, but the frank acknowledgment of it.

Youngsters cannot and should not be spared knowledge about death. When death occurs within or close to a family, no amount of caution and secrecy can hide from the children the feeling that something important and threatening has happened. They cannot avoid being affected by overtones of grief and solemnity. All the emotional reactions your youngsters are likely to have to death in the family—sorrow and loneliness, anger and rejection, guilt, anxiety about the future, and the conviction that nothing is certain or stable any more—may be considerably lessened if they feel that they know what is going on and that you are not trying to hide things from them.

You might ask, "Do you think the children should attend the funeral service of their grandfather? They loved him very dearly. They were very close to him. I'm afraid that if they go, they will become disturbed. Don't you think it would be much better if they stay with a friend during the day of the funeral?"

You expect an affirmative reply, for you intend it as a kindness when you shield them from death. You are dismayed by the suggestion that the youngsters share in the service honoring the life and memory of someone close to them. Yet recognized authorities have come to the conclusion that not only is it correct to permit children to attend a funeral, but also that if they are old enough to go to church or synagogue and can understand what is taking place, they should be offered the opportunity of *participating* in a ceremony of farewell for the loved one.

Unfortunately, many adults project their own unresolved grief upon their children. For youngsters the funeral is not bizarre and strange. A child accepts the funeral rites as a natural way of paying respect. After all, death is no stranger. In school they participate in the burial of a hamster. They witness the funerals of notables during television news programs. Funerals are popular games to play. Children love pageantry. What is a funeral but a family ceremony from the deathbed to the cemetery.

The importance of the funeral ritual is dramatically portrayed in the French film *Forbidden Games*. A girl's parents died in an air raid. She was comforted by constantly playing "the game of funeral," and providing a dead creature with an elaborate interment with casket and flowers. Playing at burying things helped her to relive, digest, and ulimately master the shock of her parents' death.

A most difficult experience is when a youth, traveling abroad, is unable to be contacted for a parent's funeral. After the young person comes home, I have noticed time and time again a denial of the reality of death. He or she was not given the opportunity of offering last respects. Often, upon return, I will accompany a youth to the cemetery for our own services of farewell. I learned this idea from the Boston psychiatrist Dr. Norman Paul and his conjoint family therapy. He discovered that incompleted grief contributed to emotional illness. Therapists may induce mourning to initiate and catalyze hidden and unresolved grief problems.

You need not delay until a person's death before you explain the meaning of a funeral. In my own temple, a funeral director is invited to explain how a funeral *may* be conducted. (I emphasize the word *may* because each funeral is indeed different, expressing respective individual needs of family members.)

Explain the purpose of the funeral and how it touches people on different levels. For the religious there is the sharing of spiritual values. However, the funeral is more than a religious event; it is also much more than the practical and legal disposing of a human body. *A funeral is for the entire community to confer group strength.* You are not alone: one touch of sorrow makes the whole world kin. You are helped from the disorganized state of shock and guilt and grief through the valley of the shadow. Your loved one has died, but friends and family still remain.

Discuss with your children what they might expect at the funeral. For example, "It will take place at a funeral home or church or synagogue. The clergyman will read appropriate prayers. Perhaps he will talk about how Grandfather touched our lives. The discussion of the things that counted in Grandfather's life will be brought out in word and song and ritual. It can be a strengthening experience for you as well as for me.

"Now, people may cry. But as we said before, what's wrong with that? It's all right. It is one of our ways of showing how much we miss him and wish to have him back. A purpose of the funeral is to provide a mode for expressing our grief."

When your youngster understands what is occurring, he may be more relaxed about the unfolding events. He understands his inclusion more than he would exclusion, and is far better off observing the funeral than living with fantasies conjured up by his young and fertile imagination.

It is difficult to determine whether an apprehensive youngster should be encouraged to attend a funeral. Certainly, he may elect to stay at home. Very often it is the parents who unconsciously make up the child's mind, saying, "You don't want to go, do you?" The decision is made not only by words but by the tone of voice. After hearing what he may expect at the ceremony, the child may change his mind many times. If the judgment is not to attend, do not place any "shaming" pressure upon him. You may gently suggest that perhaps later you may visit the cemetery together.

Don't arbitrarily send your child to stay with friends or relatives. He might construe the dismissal as another kind of abandonment or rejection. Let him know that if he desires, you would be pleased to have him remain with you. His presence could be a comfort at this difficult time. Some enlightened adults have helped a youngster feel that he has an important role to play by asking him to answer the doorbell and telephone. In this way he is given the opportunity to mingle with the family and feel needed.

Just as your children cannot be spared knowledge about death, they cannot and should not be excluded from the grief and mourning following death. They too have both a right and a need to say goodbye.

Then we went to the cemetery.

"Daddy, what's that place we're passing?"
(a cemetery)
"You're too young to understand. I'll explain it to you when you are older."

Usually, the first question a child asks when a grandfather dies is, "Where is he now?" Those with a religious orientation might express an interpretive view, but there is an answer which all can cite; namely, a factual one. You could say, "When life stopped and grandfather died, his body was placed in a casket and buried in the earth. A stone or plaque will identify the place of burial. The cemetery will be kept beautiful with flowers and shrubs. During the year, people may come to the grave to recite prayers or just to think of the person who once lived.

"Of course, not all people are buried in the earth. Some are put above the ground in a mausoleum, a building with spaces cut in the wall for crypts or vaults for the casket. And for still others, the body is burned in a place called a crematory. The ashes can be placed in a small box or urn. Or the ashes can be scattered over the ground or the ocean. Above ground, the box or urn is deposited in a space in the wall of a building called a columbarium." The technical terms however, are unimportant. What is significant is your honest, informative answers to the question: "What happened to Grandfather when he died?"

Don't wait until a person dies before you visit a cemetery. When you drive by a burial ground, and your child inquires, "What is that?" you might stop to walk through together. It is not really so traumatic for the youngster. Mystery is finally removed; shadowy ghosts replaced by real understanding.

If the child does not attend the interment service, he may come to the cemetery later with his family. This is advisable when a child cannot accept the reality of death. There is the case of a boy who was told his "mother went on a journey." He became sullen and unmanageable. Whenever the mother's name was mentioned, the child would speak of her in the vilest language. Then finally one day the child was told the truth. He was taken to the cemetery where he could visit the grave. The child was heartbroken, for he now realized that she had really died. Yet he felt better for the experience. At least, now he knew what had happened. And most important, he knew that his mother had not run out and abandoned him.

A funeral does not end in the funeral home or church or synagogue. Its logical conclusion is the grave, the mausoleum, or the columbarium where the loved one is placed. "This is what happened to Grandfather when he died; this is where he is."

Of course, we shall have grandfather in

other ways...

Tell me what you remember most about him.

We can never forget that he died.

But we will always remember

that he lived.

"I just can't wait to move out of the house. Every place reminds me of my husband. It will be better for the children and for me to get as far away as possible."

A desire to run away is natural. Your heart is heavy with the thought that the past can never return.

You then discover that there is no escape! Memories belong to the heart and mind. Ask yourself, "Why should I forget?" As children of today and tomorrow we are also children of yesterday. The past travels with us from afar and what it has been makes us what we are. There is no love without loss, no joy without sorrow.

It is not sensible to formulate quick final decisions. Too many people have left the security of familiar surroundings only to discover that problems were intensified rather than diminished. Children especially need to retain roots in the same neighborhood with their longtime playmates. Do not attempt to eradicate the memory of your loved one. Pictures are helpful for remembrance. Children may wish some tangible reminder of the deceased. They love mementos. There is an example of a young girl who was so delighted with her late grandmother's hand mirror that she treasured it for the rest of her life. Recall

59

memories of the deceased. Some people mistakenly believe
that they are most helpful when they talk about every subject
except the reason for which you have assembled; namely, that
someone has died. Encourage what Freud called the "ties of
dissolution"—that is, renewing with your child both pleasant
and unpleasant recollections. As each incident is reviewed, you
both feel anguish that an experience can never be repeated.
As pain is sustained, you gradually untie emotional bonds.

Hear what your children are really saying. If you tell your
friends you won the sweepstakes and they quietly say, "That's
nice," you are justified in thinking they care little about you.
The same is true when a bereaved person asserts, "I really feel
guilty. I should have been kinder and more compassionate"
and all you can reply is, "Just don't think or talk about it."
Cultivate the art of "listening with a third ear." Concentrate not
only on what is being said but the emotion behind it. Understand what your children need to express and what they seek
to know.

Grief shared is grief diminished. "We remember him. We can
never forget that he died. But we will always remember that
he lived."

Some Additional Thoughts
on Seeking Professional Help

---

*"My daughter is taking her father's death so terribly.
Maybe I should send her to a psychiatrist. She cries
and cries and doesn't seem to care about anything."*
"When did your husband die?"
"Two days ago."

Of course, the daughter is taking her father's death "terribly."
Death is a terrible thing for anyone. She has every right to
grieve. However, it is not the time to panic.

When should you seek some kind of counseling? Certainly
you may not be in a position to make a decision in the immediate
period following death. At this time it is so difficult to separate
the normal from the distorted. Many people say and do things
during crises that are not in keeping with their usual behavior.
Grief and sorrow leave imprints upon the healthiest of
personalities.

The line of separation between normal and distorted mourning reactions is thin indeed, like the division between normal
and neurotic actions of any kind. The difference is not in
symptom but intensity. It is *continued* denial of reality even
many months after the funeral; or *prolonged* bodily distress; or
persistent frenzy; or *extended* guilt; or *unceasing* apathy; or
enduring hostile reaction to the deceased and to others. In other
words, each manifestation does not in itself indicate a distorted
grief reaction; that can only be determined when such signs of
mourning are viewed in the total framework of behavior.

The question is not *how* is the child acting, reacting, or over-
reacting but for *how long?* After an initial period of mourning,
children are often able to work themselves back to some degree
of productive and near-normal living. Some danger signals
indicating that assistance might be considered include delinquency, unwillingness to remain in school, difficulties in
learning, sexual perversion, unreasonable withdrawal, friendless-
ness, uncommunicativeness, excessive anger, or intense
suspicion.

If there are doubts, do not hesitate to seek advice from a
therapist, psychiatrist, psychologist, child guidance clinic

(see *For Further Help* page 73). There are times when even the best-informed and well-intentioned parents are simply inadequate. Getting professional assistance is not an admission of weakness but a demonstration of real love and strength.

Reactions to the Death of a Parent

"When Grandfather died, my son didn't seem to be too affected. Now my wife has died and he can't seem to find himself."

One of the greatest difficulties for a child is the death of a parent. The world will never be as secure as before. Youngsters are deprived of attention and love they desperately need and want. "Who will take care of me now?" "Suppose something happens to you, Daddy?" "Did Mommy leave me because I was naughty?"

Anna Freud points out that a child's love for a mother becomes a pattern for all later loves: "The ability to love, like all other human faculties, has to be learned and practiced." If this relationship is interrupted through death or absence, your youngster may do one of four things: remain attached to a fantasy of the dead person; invest his love in things (or work); be frightened to love anyone but himself; or hopefully accept the loss and find another person to love.

If a boy's mother dies, he may regress. Speech becomes babyish; he sucks his thumb and whines a great deal to gain attention. He says, in effect, "Mommy, I'm only a little baby. Please, please come back and be with me." Later on in life, because he was "injured" by his mother, the prototype of all women, he may believe that all girls have a tendency to hurt him. To avoid being wounded by them, he loves and leaves them before they can do what his mother did to him: hurt and abandonment. It cannot be overemphasized, however, that these reactions need *not* occur. In most homes where there is not a mother, there are substitutes—a grandmother, housekeeper, aunt, older sister— the boy is exposed to other women.

The small boy whose father dies may feel the loss of a male person to imitate, a masculine foil to temper feelings of aggression and love. Often, the mother inadvertently contributes to the son's difficulties. Deprived of a mate, she may attempt to compensate by obtaining complete gratification from her son. Her life revolves around him and only him. Since the boy "possesses" her completely, he need not look for satisfaction elsewhere. You could cite your own examples and consequences

of doting mothers and spoiled sons. (The reverse may be observed when a mother dies and daughter and father become
inseparable.) Big Brothers or Big Sisters would be excellent
organizations to contact for help in this situation.

Avoid the temptation of making the child a surrogate partner.
Your youngster does not replace the absent mate. Physical
intimacy such as sharing a bedroom should be tactfully avoided.
Seductive and sexually stimulating situations cause embarrass-
ment and guilt. Your child is not your lover, companion, con-
fessor, spouse. Children should be accepted within the confines
of their psychological and intellectual capabilities and limita-
tions. They are still youngsters and have their own difficult
grief reactions to a parent's death to deal with.

The Child's Loss of a Brother or Sister

"Now that the older child has died, the younger one just doesn't seem the same anymore."

Life is never the same after a death. The loss has affected both you and your relationship with your remaining children. You may be so absorbed in your own grief that you just cannot share together as a family unit. Or you may be turning more closely and protectively to your surviving youngsters. In the words of the Society of the Compassionate Friends, "there is no death so saddening as the loss of your beloved child."

A child's reaction to the death of a sibling may be the frightening realization that it could happen to her. After all, she is part of the same biological inheritance. "Is something also wrong with me?" she may think but never put into words. "Will I die when I reach my brother's age?" Youngsters may assume babyish behavior to magically prevent themselves from growing old and dying. Parents should say again and again, "You are fine. There is nothing wrong with you. You do not have the disease that caused your brother's death."

Seeing the grieving parents, a child may try to replace the deceased brother or sister and make everything all right again. Adults sometimes unconsciously promote this kind of behavior by saying, "You know you are so much like him in so many ways." You are only hurting yourself and your living child. As difficult as it is to accept, you must now understand that one of your youngsters *is* dead. The child cannot be resurrected in the form of someone else who has his or her own way of life. Let the dead lie in peace. Do not make comparisons. Your child has enough difficulties without having to assume a new identity.

The surviving child is often beset with guilt. He or she remembers the times when they fought and argued. He or she recalls past anger and jealousy. "Is death a punishment for my wrongdoing?" he or she may wonder. Listen to your youngsters' fears. Let them know that nothing they said or did caused the death. Even with the terrible loss, you are still a family. Your love for one another is not lost.

When Suicide Occurs

"My husband took his life. Our son keeps saying, 'Maybe Daddy was angry with me.'"

Surviving children of a suicidal parent have special problems in coping with the tragedy. The statement, "You did nothing to make him die . . . all people die," could appear mocking. Of course everyone eventually dies. In the case of suicide, however, the person deliberately took his or her own life! There is a far greater burden of guilt and anger. Because of the social stigma, the youngster may carry the bitter experience for the rest of his or her life.

The child may ask, "What did I do wrong? Did he commit suicide because I was bad and mean to him? Did he not love me enough to want to live?" Death by suicide brings the greatest of all affronts to those who remain.

It is of no help to say, "Don't talk about it." The child is going through an intense emotional crisis. He or she needs to articulate and act out reactions—denial, turning slowly to bewilderment, and finally to the weeping, despairing confrontation with the truth of the suicide. The bereaved need to pour out their hearts.

A most important way you can encourage this grief work is by responsive listening. Your son may tell you that he was cast in the same mold as the parent. He constantly recalls similarities, how they resembled one another both physically and mentally. Help the youngster understand the truth. There is no cruel seed of self-destruction lurking in him. The person who died is not the same person as the child who is beside you. Each individual is different. No two people are exactly alike. Suicidal tendencies are not bequeathed like family heirlooms.

Nor does it help to say that the one who took his life must have been out of his mind. The term "crazy" does not lighten the blow. Nor is it often the truth. To quote Schneidman, Faberow, and Litman: "The majority of persons who commit suicide are tormented and ambivalent; they may be neurotic or have character disorders, but *they are not insane.*" Telling survivors that the deceased was out of his mind does not comfort them; it only brings out the fear of inherited disease. The child may think, "I am his child; I must be crazy too."

You might add, "There is much that we do not know about

suicide. At that moment, death was his way of handling his troubled life. But you are not your father. Suicide is not inherited. You will learn that there are other ways to work through problems."

Conversation should be natural. Interest should be genuine and sincere. Don't try too hard. Oversolicitation engenders suspicion and guilt reactions. You are not to justify or to censure. Rather together, adult and child, you will try to build the temple of tomorrow's dreams upon the grave of yesterday's bitterness.

For Adults Only

This book is not solely for children. It is also for you the parents. What you are will determine what you teach your youngsters. Your attitudes are being absorbed by your offspring. If you are unable to talk about death, they too will probably remain silent. If you conceal your emotions, they too may repress their fear, guilt, and confusion. In short, not only children but adults must now face the fact that death *is* part of life.

Easier said than done. Your loved one is dead. It is final and irrevocable. You have feelings of sorrow, anxiety, uncertainty about the future. You can't help thinking: "If only I had had a few more hours with him [or her]. If only I had treated that person a little bit better, If only . . . if only." You keep remembering all the things you wanted to say and do but didn't. Now it is too late.

Your friends may try to help you but often in vain. There is little consolation in knowing that countless others have suffered similar losses. You boil inside when people tell you now well you are doing. How do they know the flood of emotions that are tormenting you? The ridiculous clichés—"It's all for the best." "It's God's will." "He lived to a ripe old age"—all this does not bring a healing balm when at the moment the pain of separation appears irreparable. When you hear the oft-repeated phrase, "I know just how you feel," you want to scream, "No, you don't! How can you possibly know how I really feel?"

You are in a state of shock. How do you accept the unacceptable? You are overwhelmed with self-pity, self-doubt, estrangement from people, and loneliness. Your feelings are numbed as you go through mechanical motions of life. You are anxious and insecure about the future. "What will happen to me?"

Do you feel better if you cry? "Certainly not in front of the children," you say. Why not? Your secure, well-ordered world has crumpled. Release your feelings rather than nurse them. Emotions should be accepted for what they are. No family cover-up campaign. How terrible it would be to have no emotions.

Life is not "fair"; you must find a way of living with an unfair life. You continue to exist. Not like before; not the way you would decide if you had a choice. There are times when you are not sure that it is all worth it. You wish you were dead. You feel as though you are losing your mind. Yet, you continue to survive. You are confronted with the seemingly bitter fact that you are destined to go on living. In the words of Edna St. Vincent Millay: "Life goes on . . . I forget just why."

Then somehow you begin to take yourself in hand. You accept the consolation and love of your family and friends. You learn the sad truth that most people do not wish to hear of your continuing grief. If, however, you have one close friend with whom you may share your feelings, you are truly fortunate. You are not alone. There are many fine organizations (see *For Further Help*) that will assist you when your so-called "good friends" have left the cemetery. There are books (see *For Further Reading* . . .) that will afford new insights.

You continue to ask, "Why did this happen to me? The funeral is over, but I am not getting any better. Who says that time heals?" There is a silent, knifelike terror that keeps recurring. You are not only grieving for the person who died but for yourself, your sense of loss. You keep telling yourself that you *must* face life without your loved one.

Psychologists call this approach "withdrawing the emotional capital of the past." You do not disregard the person who died. Memories should never be forgotten. But you realize that yesterday with its joys and sorrows has ended. All that it holds of your life is in the treasure-house of the past. There are beautiful reminiscences—sweet and tender. They were yours, but now they are over.

An effective way of breaking the tie is by refusing to create a memorial shrine. Certainly, pictures and mementos can be retained as a visual, tangible reminder of days gone by. It is not necessary, however, to keep the person's clothes intact in the closet (in the secret hope that the individual will someday return). It is within the highest humanitarian traditions to give clothing to the Salvation Army, Good Will Industries, or any organization dedicated to relieve the plight of the poor and needy. A world of caution: you may not wish to make donations to someone in the immediate vicinity. What a shocking experience to witness a neighbor who in the clothes of the deceased for a brief moment becomes a "reincarnation" of your loved one. Furniture may also be rearranged. The goal is to strike that delicate balance between the past that should be remembered and a future that must be created.

As the weeks go by, the depth of sorrow diminishes slowly and at times imperceptibly. You are doing things you never thought possible. You are discovering hidden capabilities you had never before tapped. (The average healthy individual often functions at less than ten percent of his or her potential.) Simple things: a husband learns how to work the washing machine for the first time; a wife tries to balance the checkbook and after fruitless and frustrating attempts finally succeeds. A sense of inner satisfaction emerges. You say: "I never did it before. I never thought I could. But I did it *myself*." You are growing in the ability to make decisions. You are withdrawing your dependence, declaring your independence, and planning for the future.

Later, your mind is recovering from its numbed state. You are seeking new interests, satisfactions, creative activities. You are experimenting with undeveloped talent and potential. Perhaps you will begin the music lessons you always wanted to take . . . or further schooling . . . or the hobby you had always wished you could master.

Feelings are marvelously released through artistic media. One mother provided finger paints for her son so he could express his mood. The two worked together, talking as they painted. The mother later remarked that the hour was as helpful for her as for her child. One man expressed his feelings by playing selections with crashing chords and dissonances on the piano.

Another way of coping is by physical activity. You immerse yourself completely working in the garden . . . you release excess energy by playing tennis, golf, walking, or jogging. (Of course you should make sure you have a medical checkup before doing a strenuous sport.)

There are organizations, clubs, hospitals, charities, church, and civic groups that desperately need your help and talents. What a meaningful way to take your mind off yourself and your own anxieties. New relationships are formed, new acquaintances made, new challenges developed. In the beginning you literally had to force yourself to leave the security of your home. In the end you lift up your own spirits as you lend a hand to another.

One danger. Some, in the desperate search for distraction at any cost, become involved in the headlong flight into endless activity. This frenzy offers but a temporary relaxation of tension. The effort becomes abortive, for you soon grow weary from physical fatigue and disenchanted with sporadic causes. Remember, any medicine taken to excess becomes poison.

You will find that you occasionally need to be by yourself. Solitude is not necessarily loneliness. It is good to have time to think and take stock of your life. In solitude you cry and remember, but you also dream and hope. Since life is no longer

the same, you formulate new philosophies of life. Self-aware-
ness leads to understanding and recognition of your best
potential. Psychiatrist Avery Weisman points out that, unless
a person's way of life is broad enough to confront his own death
of those close to him, he has an inadequate perspective of life.
Grief is a strange mixture of joy and sorrow—joy to be alive
and sorrow to have life diminished by the loss of the one you
love.

Just when you think you are making great strides forward
and you are coping well, you receive a startling setback. You
think you are back where you started when your loved one had
just died. Realize that difficulty is not the same as defeat.
Progress is almost always slow. You will have slips and spills
before your footing becomes firmer, but slowly, slowly you will
rebuild your world.

The most important gift you can give your children at this
time is the feeling that life continues despite pain. Death, "the
loss of innocence," can either lead you to the edge of the abyss
and threaten your existence with meaninglessness and futility;
or you will start to build the bridge that spans the chasm with
things of life that still count—memory, family, friendship, love.
When you have sorted out your own feelings, you will be better
able to understand your troubled children who come to you
laden with questions and beset with fears. This is the reason
why this book is not solely for children. It is for you the parents
as well. The real challenge is not just how to explain death to
children but how to make peace with it yourself.

FOR FURTHER HELP

CLERGY AND RELIGIOUS AGENCIES

The concerned religious community offers a society bound together by ties of sympathy, love, and mutual concern. Fellowships of church, synagogue, and religious organizations are networks of meaningful relationships that could be the difference between your coping with or collapsing under the pressure of loss.

Your first call might be to the person who officiated at the funeral. The minister has no knowledge of your problems unless you have shared your feelings. A pastor could be of great help by offering insights about the anxieties of loneliness, guilt, and suffering.

The following religious organizations and agencies may also be of assistance:

American Association of Pastoral Counselors
3 West 29th Street
New York, New York 10001

Department of Family Ministries
National Council of Churches
475 Riverside Drive
New York, New York 10027

An excellent *Marriage and Family Life Newsletter* cites useful material on the many ways Protestant churches are helping families that have experienced bereavement. The Council also publishes a helpful pamphlet, "Interpreting Death to Children," by Helen and Lewis Sherrill.

Fellowship of Christian Widows
1439 Almeria Drive
Hayward, California 94544

"At a very crucial time we extend to the widow our Christian friendship and concern." Services are educational, inspirational, and social through rap sessions, coffee klatches, dinner parties, and weekend trips. The Fellowship publishes a pamphlet by Lucille Rose, "Not a Fifth Wheel."

Jewish Big Brother Association
72 Franklin Street
Boston, Massachusetts 02110

The Association renders a unique service by supplying a mature male adult for a Jewish boy who does not have a father to guide him. Activities include a variety of recreational, cultural, and educational events. Counseling available for the mother. Other organizations in Baltimore, Cleveland, Los Angeles, and New York.

Jewish Widows and Widowers
Beth El Temple Center
2 Concord Avenue
Belmont, Massachusetts 02178

How to adjust to a new life with children, in-laws, friends, job, daily routine. The Jewish widows and widowers share the burden of meeting the problems of widowhood.

NAIM Conference
109 North Dearborn Street
Chicago, Illinois 60602

With more than thirty chapters, the well-planned programs cover the educational, spiritual, and social needs of the widowed.

NAIM Conference
2021 N. 60th Street
Milwaukee, Wisconsin 53208

Under the spiritual leadership of the Reverend Donald N. Weber, the purpose of the Catholic Family Life Program is "to aid the adjustment of those spiritual, psychological, financial, social, and family problems that arise either directly or indirectly from the death of a husband or wife." There is also a group for parents under 45.

THEOS Foundation
11609 Frankstown Road
Pittsburgh, Pennsylvania 15235

In 1962 a young widow, Mrs. Beatrice Decker, founded THEOS—the Greek word for "God" and an acronym for "They Help Each Other Spiritually." There are now over 21 chapters throughout the United States and Canada. A program for the young and middle-aged widowed and the "lonely who need to know someone really cares, the troubled who require a helping hand."

Widow and Widower Outreach Program
Jewish Family Service Agency
1600 Scott Street
San Francisco, California 94115

A program where widow aides call on recently widowed
Jewish people. Under staff sponsorship, the agency leads discussion groups. Social activities are also part of program.

For an understanding of the theological concepts of death of
Catholicism, Protestantism, and Judaism, refer to chapters by
Bishop Thomas J. Riley, the Reverend Dr. Edgar N. Jackson,
and Rabbi Dr. Earl A. Grollman in *Explaining Death To
Children* (7, 8, 9, Beacon Press, 1967, edited by Earl A. Grollman).

For more practical understanding of the various faiths' respective customs for the funeral, visitation, and condolence call,
and recommended expressions of sorrow, see Chapters 5, 6, 7 in
Concerning Death: A Practical Guide for the Living (Beacon
Press, 1974, edited by Earl A. Grollman).

GUIDANCE AND FAMILY ASSOCIATIONS

American Association of Marriage
and Family Counselors
225 Yale Avenue
Claremont, California 91711

The Association is concerned not just with marriage counseling but also with the needs and problems of the total family.
The three thousand members include psychologists, psychiatrists,
social workers, and clergy, trained to help those who have
sustained a death in the family.

Family Service Association of America
44 East 23rd Street
New York, New York 10010

The motto: "Strength to Families Under Stress" is a real-life
experience to more than two million annually. The Association
conducts a major program of family counseling for child care
and personal development. The purpose is to enable families
to help themselves.

National Association for Mental Health
1800 North Kent Street
Arlington, Virginia 22209

A national voluntary citizens' organization working through
41 state associations to combat mental illness and promote
mental health. The Association provides person-to-person help

through information services for local resources as well as special treatment and school service programs for emotionally disturbed children.

National Association of Social Workers
1425 H Street, N.W.
Washington, D.C. 20005

Trained social workers have come into their own as counselors for people in crisis. Many work within the context of child guidance clinics and comprehensive mental health centers.

National Council on Family Relations
1219 University Avenue, S.E.
Minneapolis, Minnesota 55414

Founded in 1938 as an interprofessional forum through which members of many disciplines work and plan together for the strengthening of family life. An important concern is death education as part of family-life understanding.

OTHER ORGANIZATIONS

There are a variety of self-help groups and organizations devoted to helping children and their parents through crises.

American Association of Retired Persons
1909 K Street, N.W.
Washington, D.C. 20049

An excellent division for widowed persons is "Action for Independent Maturity" in Morris County, New Jersey; Tulsa, Oklahoma; Atlanta, Georgia; and Washington, D.C. The association publishes a helpful brochure, *On Being Alone.*

The American National Red Cross
National Headquarters
Washington, D.C. 20006

This emergency-oriented organization helps individuals, families, and communities cope with crisis. In case of death there are services to members of the armed forces and their families. For the child who has sustained a loss and does not know how to fill his or her free time the Youth Service Programs have accommodated more than six million young people in worthwhile programs.

Big Brothers of America
220 Suburban Station Building
Philadelphia, Pennsylvania 19103

With more than 235 local member agencies the Big Brothers has helped thousands of boys who have no father with whom to identify.

Big Sisters
220 Suburban Station Building
Philadelphia, Pennsylvania 19103

The group is especially recommended for the widower who feels that his daughter should have the companionship of an older female volunteer.

National Foundation for Sudden Infant Death
1501 Broadway
New York, New York 10036

Sudden Infant Death Syndrome (SIDS) commonly known as "crib death" is a disease which causes about ten thousand infant deaths annually. Local chapters respond to such painful questions as "Was it my fault?"—"Did my baby suffocate in its bedding?"—"Could my infant have vomited and choked after the last feeding?"—"Could it have been prevented?" In addition to intervening on behalf of stricken parents most SIDS chapters offer professional counseling services for adults and children.

N.O.W. National Office
5 South Wabash, Suite 1615
Chicago, Illinois 60603

For the widow or widower with a child, the National Organization for Women has dedicated itself to the creation of high quality developmental child care programs. "The centers are available to all citizens on the same basis as public schools, parks, and libraries; adequate to the needs of children from preschool age through adolescence as well as to the needs of their parents."

Parents Without Partners
7910 Woodmont Avenue
Washington, D.C. 20014

An international nonprofit, nonsectarian organization with a membership of eighty thousand in over six hundred chapters concerned with the welfare of single parents and their children.

The Society of the Compassionate Friends
Post Office Box 3247
Hialeah, Florida 33013

An international organization of bereaved parents who have been through their own time of loneliness and isolation, and seek to help relieve the mental anguish of other families whose child has died.

United Way of America
801 North Fairfax Street
Alexandria, Virginia 22314

The Information and Referral Service helps bereaved parents

and children find an appropriate agency. It could be a family service association, a children's camp, a Big Brothers or Big Sisters organization, a mental health facility, a child guidance clinic, or a social service.

PHYSICIANS

The family doctor knows the patient through years of personal medical service and has a unique opportunity to observe physical and emotional health. More important than possible medicine prescribed are the insights offered by the family doctor.

For information, write:

American Academy of Family Physicians
1740 West 92nd Street
Kansas City, Missouri 64114

or

The American Medical Association
535 North Dearborn Street
Chicago, Illinois 60610

PSYCHOLOGICAL AND PSYCHIATRIC SERVICES

Below are three major national psychological and psychiatric associations with accredited professionals and services:

Psychological: American Psychological Association
1200 17th Street, N.W.
Washington, D.C. 20036

Psychiatric: American Psychiatric Association
1700 18th Street, N.W.
Washington, D.C. 20009

American Psychoanalytic Association
1 East 57th Street
New York, New York 10022

SCHOOL COUNSELING DEPARTMENTS

When a death occurs, it is suggested that you call your children's school counseling service. The school environment often becomes the focus of children's grief. A study of 49 bereaved students conducted in the Arlington, Massachusetts, public schools shows that the majority of pupils had difficulty concentrating on their lessons. Not only did grade performance decline, but many had trouble in relating to peer groups. Others demanded a great deal of attention from puzzled teachers, who had never been informed of the family situation.

Most communities have a coordinated counseling service for students from kindergarten level through high school. Counseling is the core of a guidance department. Inform the department of the death in the family and the manner your youngsters seem to relate to the loss. The counselor could help to further identify the emotional difficulties that may not only adversely affect educational development but mental health as well. Through personal interviews, contact with teachers, and appropriate testing, the guidance department may better assist the youngsters toward self-understanding in meeting their special emergency. Referrals to professional agencies may be in order if circumstances warrant. In short, the school counseling service could be an invaluable resource during your children's crisis.

WIDOW-TO-WIDOW PROJECTS

Emotional breakdowns among widows, especially in younger age groups, present a substantial problem that few in America are trained to prevent. Recognizing the special needs of the newly bereaved, Dr. Phyllis R. Silverman, psychiatric social worker, and Dr. Gerald Caplan, of the Laboratory of Community Psychiatry of Harvard Medical School, started the Widow-to-Widow Project in 1967. The emphasis is on self-help groups in which the primary caregiver is another widowed person. The concern and goal are to stimulate programs of preventive intervention. The program has grown nationally; the following are but a random sample:

> Connecticut Council—Widows Widowers Associated
> 60 Lorraine Street
> Hartford, Connecticut 06105

With other nonsectarian chapters in Norwalk, Waterbury, Bridgeport, New Haven, and Danbury, their purpose is "to bring together the widowed in fellowship, to help them find a new way of life, to assure them that they are not alone, and to develop a public awareness and recognition of the needs of the widowed." Their motto is "Sharing by Caring."

> Family Service of Westchester, Inc.
> 470 Mamaroneck Avenue
> White Plains, New York 10605

The nonsectarian agency has developed the Widow and Widower Club with membership for Westchester County. Coordinated by a trained social worker, the emphasis is on individual counseling, small discussion groups, community education, and an outreach program to help the newly bereaved.

79

Widows Consultation Center
136 East 57th Street
New York, New York 10022

The Center is a nonprofit, nonsectarian agency offering information, counseling, and advisory services to widows on an individual or group basis. "In addition to coping with grief and loneliness the widow may have to adjust to a new and difficult role—that of the single parent. She has to accept the weight of added responsibilities while overwhelmed with feelings of dependency, of fear of being a burden to her children. She may feel neglected or may look to her children for emotional support they cannot give."

Widow to Widow Program
69 Summer Street
Haverhill, Massachusetts 01830

The program is based on the premise that another widow is the best person to reach out to a bereaved woman. Regarded as an intervention service, volunteers are also especially interested in reaching out to the children.

Widow to Widowed Program
Needham Community Council
51 Lincoln Street
Needham, Massachusetts 02192

Patterned on the program of the Harvard Medical School of Community Psychiatry, the Needham program is also a self-help approach in preventive intervention. Trained widowed volunteers reach out on a one-to-one basis to recently widowed men and women, offering support in adjusting to their new life.

Widowed to Widowed Program of San Diego
6655 Alvarado Road
San Diego, California 92120

Through this program trained "widowed visitors" contact and offer emotional support to the newly widowed. A 24-hour hotline together with ongoing classes and problem-solving discussions are offered to the bereaved and their families.

For further information, consult:
Dr. Phyllis R. Silverman
Laboratory of Community Psychiatry
Harvard Medical School
58 Fenwood Road
Boston, Massachusetts 02115

FOR FURTHER READING, LISTENING, AND VIEWING

Facing the Other Part of Life:
Death in Children's Literature

Examine a child's book dealing with death and you will quickly understand how the concept of separation was viewed by the adult world at the time the book was written.

Many years ago death was a customary aspect of life. With a high mortality rate, death was a frequent visitor. In the *New England Primer* published in 1788 are the words:

> In the burying place you may see
> Graves shorter there than I
> From death's arrest, no age is free
> Young children too may die.

Early literature alluded to death with an almost obsessive preoccupation. In modern times, an about-face; there has been an unhealthy avoidance of the inevitable.

Today, the average child born in America might expect to live to about 72, fully 25 years longer than he or she probably would have at the turn of the century. Previously, multitudes could be expected to die in the home of bacterial pneumonia, diphtheria, and poliomyelitis. With antibiotics, vaccines, and improved sanitation, the once lethal effects of these maladies have been virtually eliminated. Since our ancestors were in constant touch with death, they were compelled to view it as a natural phenomenon.

In our own time until very recently the idea of death has

either been avoided and/or camouflaged. We have talked not about the death of real people but the death of disease through organ transplantation and hemodialysis. Death has been an obscenity not to be discussed or even mentioned. There has been a superstitious belief that if not talked about, it would simply disappear. Death itself would "pass away." It is what some social scientists call "the dying of death."

As a result there has been a reluctance on the part of parents to share the experience of death with their children. This accounts for the former dearth of material for the child. Ms. Joanne Gard Marshall of the Biomedical Library, McMaster University, wrote of "the inadequate number of titles suitable for the younger reader."

Fortunately in the past few years there has been a noticeable change. The area of death and dying has become a respectable concern for the health professional and social scientist. Instead of pretending that death is not a basic condition of life, the theme of death is now included in the curricula of hundreds of elementary grades, high schools, and universities. Children's writers are not only talking about the biological processes surrounding the beginning of existence, they are beginning to discuss the evidence of the end of the life cycle as well. From these new resources has come a maturity of spirit that not only understands the purpose of life but accepts the mystery of death.

A word of caution. Before you direct your child to a book from this list, read the book first for yourself. Do you think that the "sand-dobby" concept in Coburn's book will confuse your child? Is the tenth good thing about Barney, namely, that the boy's cat "will change until he's part of the ground" and "help grow flowers," really consoling? Do you agree with the Christian tone and suggestion of immortality in Picard's story of King Arthur?

Should the book be about a dead bird or a real person? And who is the individual who has died—a grandparent, parent, sibling, or friend? Did the person die of natural causes or by accident? Is the main character in the story a boy or girl with whom your child could identify? To better aid you in your selection a brief description follows each recommended book.

The age categories for the bibliography are meant to serve only as a general guide. For example, E. B. White's *Charlotte's Web* has been placed in fiction for the middle grades, yet many have found it ideal for a read-aloud to fairly mature 7–8-year-olds. There are, of course, developmental differences even for youngsters of the same age, so take time to decide which books may be most useful. As your children learn of life from the books they read, so may they learn of death which is the other part of life.

Preschool to Age 8

Brown, Margaret W., *The Dead Bird* (New York: Young Scott Books, 1958).

In finding a bird, still warm but dead, a little girl and her playmates meet death for the first time. In a poignant episode they accept the finality of death with a funeral and burial. "And every day, until they forgot, they went and sang to their dead bird and put fresh flowers on his grave."

dePaoloa, Tomie, *Nana Upstairs and Nana Downstairs* (New York: G. P. Putnam's Sons, 1973).

This is a quiet story of the wonderful times that Tommy shares with his greatgrandmother (Nana Upstairs) and his grandmother (Nana Downstairs). Each dies, but lives on in memories.

Dobrin, Arnold, *Scat* (New York: Four Winds Press, 1971).

Scott, who lives in turn-of-the-century New Orleans, is a jazz musician. This angers his grandmother. When Grandma dies, Scott heeds her final advice to ". . . listen to what your heart says . . . not your head." So he chooses his own way to say goodbye. At her grave he plays the blues on his harmonica.

Fassler, Joan, *My Grandpa Died Today* (New York: Behavioral Publications, Inc., 1971).

A tender story of a love shared by a young boy and his grandfather. When the grandfather dies, the boy is comforted when he realizes that despite his pain, he has "to go right on playing and reading, and running, and laughing, and growing up."

Harris, Audrey, *Why Did He Die?* (Minneapolis: Lerner Publications Company, 1965).

A small child wrestles with the concept of his grandfather's death. Is he dead for good? Why can't he live forever? What is a cemetery? Finally he understands: "He won't forget his granddad, but now it's time to play!"

Kantorowitz, Mildred, *When Violet Died* (New York: Parent's Magazine Press, 1973).

Violet, a parakeet, dies. A youngster learns that nothing lasts forever, but there is comfort in the continuity of life exemplified by the children's pregnant cat.

Martin, Patricia M., *John Fitzgerald Kennedy* (New York: G. P. Putnam's Sons, 1964).

A picture book of the life and death of the former President. There is a particularly vivid account of the assassination and funeral. Very popular with 2nd–4th graders for reading on their own.

Miles, Miska, *Annie and the Old One* (Boston: Little, Brown and Company, 1971).

A beautiful story of a little Indian girl who is given a weaving stick by her dying grandmother. The Old One will die when the rug has been woven. To postpone her grandmother's death, the girl undoes the weaving. The Old One explains that one cannot change the order of nature. The story ends with the grandchild taking her place at the loom. Death occurs; life goes on.

Viorst, Judith, *The Tenth Good Thing About Barney* (New York: Atheneum, 1971).

When Barney the cat dies, his young owner tries to think of ten good things to say at the funeral. He can only think of nine. While helping his father in the garden, he discovers the tenth good thing—Barney will now help things grow. A warm, honest, sensitive response to the death of a pet.

Warburg, Sandol S., *Growing Time* (Boston: Houghton Mifflin Company, 1969).

After Jamie's dog dies, the young boy finally begins to accept the loss with the help of his understanding family. The book treats the youngster's feelings with dignity and does not resort to facile consolations.

Zolotow, Charlotte, *My Grandson Lew* (New York: Harper, 1974).

Before the story begins, Lew's grandfather has died. Lew misses Grandpa, whose "beard scratched" when he kissed and who would comfort Lew after a bad dream. What makes the story so tender is the loving relationship in which the small child can share his memories with his mother.

Middle Grades: Ages 8–11

Alcott, Louisa M., *Little Men* (New York: The Macmillan Company, 1963).

Thirteen boys make Plumfield House ring with the sounds of laughter and tears. In the afterword, Clifton Fadiman writes, "The most moving episode has to do with John Brooke's death and funeral. As I read it, I found myself wondering why most books for children these days are afraid to mention death."

Alcott, Louisa M., *Little Women* (New York: World, 1969).

Generations of young people have had their first vicarious experience with death and grief through *Little Women*. In the classic story of New England life in the early 1900s, Beth, one of the four March sisters, dies, surrounded by dear ones. The family is very real, the death is very real, and the effects it has on the survivors are treated skillfully. Especially popular with 4th–8th-grade girls.

Beim, Jerrold, *With Dad Alone* (New York: Harcourt, Brace, and Company, 1954).

Several of the previous books deal with the death of a grandparent or father. In this story it is the mother who dies. The boy must now assume some new duties such as helping with his younger brothers.

Buck, Pearl S., *The Big Wave* (New York: The John Day Company, 1947).

When Jiya's parents die in a tidal wave, his foster father, with wisdom and tenderness, helps him to accept the tragedy. Japanese philosophy is explained: one is placed on earth not to fear death but to make the most out of life. "To live in the presence of death makes us brave and strong . . . to die a little later—a little sooner—does not matter. What matters is to live."

Cleaver, Vera and Bill, *Grover* (Philadelphia: J. B. Lippincott Company, 1970).

Eleven-year-old Grover's dying mother has shot and killed herself. Is it an accident? In a burst of rage, Grover takes revenge by killing a turkey, but finds no relief. Finally, through terrible pain he begins to mature and face life.

Coburn, John B., *Anne and the Sand Dobbies* (New York: The Seabury Press, 1964).

"This is the story about my sister, Anne, who died. It's also the story of Bonnie, my dog, who died too—or rather got killed." With the help of an adult friend and mythical sand dobbies the boy reaches an understanding of what it means to die.

Cohen, Barbara, *Thank You, Jackie Robinson* (New York: Lothrop, Lee and Shepard, 1974).

Twelve-year-old Sam and the elderly Black cook, Davy, both share a deep interest in sports, especially in the late Jackie Robinson. When Davy suffers a fatal heart attack, the reader identifies and sympathizes with Sam's intense feelings of grief.

Corley, Elizabeth A., *Tell Me About Death. Tell Me About Funerals* (Santa Clara, California: Grammatical Sciences, 1973).

A child learns firsthand of the intricate details of what happens when his grandfather dies. What is a funeral home, an embalmer, casket, pallbearers, hearse, mausoleum? His parents comfort him: "You miss him very much, but you can still think about him and you can still love him."

Kipling, Rudyard, *The Jungle Book* (Garden City, New York: Doubleday, 1964).

Mowgli, lost in the jungle of India as a baby, is brought up by wolves and becomes an integral part of the animal life about him. A description of the impartial law of nature. The one who obeys the law of the jungle survives; the one who errs, dies.

L'Engle, Madeleine, *Meet The Austins* (New York: The Vanguard Press, 1960).

Maggy, a child orphaned when her father is killed in a plane crash, comes to live with the Austins. She is insolent and sullen. Eventually Maggy accepts the loss, aided by the warmth and security of the Austin family.

Picard, Barbara L., *Stories of King Arthur and His Knights* (New York: Oxford Press, 1955).

Like Oedipus, Arthur's death is the result of his own unwitting sin. The myth, rich in symbolism, is popular with many youths. The whole Arthurian cycle is Christian in tone and immortality is suggested.

Smith, Doris B., *A Taste of Blackberries* (New York: Thomas Y. Crowell, 1973).

Jamie fooled around a lot. When he rolled on the ground after a bee sting, his friend thought he was joking. But Jamie died and the friend felt guilty and responsible. At the funeral, Jamie "didn't look like he was asleep . . . Jamie looked dead." In this Child Study Association Award-winning book, the friend finally accepts this terrible tragedy.

White E.B., *Charlotte's Web* (New York: Harper and Row, 1952).

An animal fantasy. When Charlotte, the spider, dies at the fairgrounds, her friends, Templeton, the rat, and Wilbur, the pig, manage to take her eggs back to the farm where they could safely hatch. The friends understand that no one can ever replace Charlotte's special quality of friendship. For reading to the 6–8-year-olds, or for 8–12-year-olds to read by themselves.

Whitehead, Ruth, *The Mother Tree* (New York: The Seabury Press, 1971).

The story of a ten-year-old girl whose mother dies suddenly. She now is required to help with the household chores as well as take care of her clinging four-year-old sister, who continually asks, "When will Mother be home again?" A moving experience of how the girls spend the summer with their grandmother.

Windsor, Patricia, *The Summer Before* (New York: Harper and Row, 1973).

A journal of an adolescent girl's reactions to her boyfriend's accidental death. As a result of therapy, she accepts the situation and looks forward to the future.

Zim, Herbert S., and Sonia Bleeker, *Life and Death* (New York: William Morrow and Company, 1970).

In a straightforward approach the writers discuss the physical facts, customs, and attitudes surrounding death. The various rites that constitute funeral and burial procedures are described and compared with those of other cultures.

Grades 7 (age 12) and up

Agee, James, *A Death in the Family* (New York: Avon, 1959).

The Pulitzer Prize winner describes death as an inseparable part of human experience. A novel of overwhelming sensitivity and compassion about how a family and a six-year-old boy, Rufus Follet, respond to the death of a father.

Brown, John M., *Morning Faces* (New York: McGraw-Hill Book Company, 1949).

Various sketches describe the excitement, disappointment, surprises, and joys of being the parents of two small boys. In the chapter

"The Long Shadow" the author reveals the depth of understanding of an eleven-year-old boy who asserts, "I don't like God anymore . . . why should I? Now that He has done this to my father." The conclusion is that though death is final, memories have a life of their own.

Buck, Pearl S., *The Good Earth* (New York: The John Day Company, 1931).

In an almost pastoral style, the book beautifully describes the cycle of birth, marriage, and death in a Chinese peasant family during the early twentieth century.

Cleaver, Vera and Bill, *Where the Lilies Bloom* (Philadalphia: J.B. Lippincott Company, 1969).

After the death of both of her parents, a fourteen-year-old Appalachian girl helps her three siblings struggle to survive a long, bitter winter. In a moving tribute to human endurance, the children manage to stay together and help one another.

Crane, Stephen, *Red Badge of Courage* (New York: Random House, 1951).

The personal reactions of a young recruit during the Civil War. Henry Fleming soon learns the meaning of battle and death. Soldiers are not always motivated by unselfish heroism but more often by fear and egoism.

Craven, Margaret, *I Heard The Owl Call My Name* (Garden City, New York: Doubleday and Company, 1973).

With three years to live, a 27-year-old Anglican missionary is sent to an Indian village in Canada. He finally understands the real meaning of life and death.

Dooley, Thomas A., *Doctor Tom Dooley, My Story* (New York: Farrar, Strauss and Company, 1960).

The personal account of Dr. Dooley before his death at the age of 34. "The jagged, ugly cancer scar went no deeper than my flesh. There was no cancer in my spirit."

Frank, Anne, *The Diary of a Young Girl* (New York: Washington Square Press, 1963).

A moving autobiography of a twelve-year-old Jewish girl who lives with seven other people in a single nest of rooms in Amsterdam during the Nazi occupation. Anne died, but her diary lives.

Gunther, John, *Death Be Not Proud: A Memoir* (New York: Harper, 1949).

The author writes of the courage with which his seventeen-year-old son faces a premature death from a brain tumor. A classic that was made into a television program.

Hemingway, Ernest, *A Farewell to Arms* (New York: Charles Scribner's Sons, 1929).

Hemingway combines austere realism and poetic language with a moving story of war, love, and death. Who will forget the startling conclusion with Lieutenant Frederic Henry's learning of Catherine's hemorrhaging: "I went into the room and stayed with Catherine until she died. She was unconscious all the time, and it did not take her very long to die . . . After a while I went out and left the hospital and walked back to the hotel in the rain."

Klein, Norma, *Sunshine* (New York: Avon, 1974).
Based on the real-life diaries and tapes of a dying nineteen-year-old youth.

L'Engle, Madeleine, *A Wrinkle in Time* (New York: Farrar, Strauss, and Giroux, 1962).
A science fiction story of good versus evil and life versus death. Three children pass through time and defeat "IT" with their chants of love.

Levit, Rose, *Ellen: A Short Life Long Remembered* (San Francisco: Chronicle Books, 1974).
Ellen's exceptional promise could not be realized. At the age of fifteen, her life is ending. Through her own poems as well as her mother's narrative Ellen's story is a testimonial to the strength of the human spirit.

Miller, Arthur, *Death of a Salesman* (New York: The Viking Press, 1949).
The story of Willy Loman blends the themes of social and personal tragedy. His downfall and final defeat illustrate not only the failure of a man but also the failure of a way of life.

Mohr, Nicholasa, *Nilda* (New York: Harper and Row, 1973).
A very personal story of a 10–12-year-old Puerto Rican girl surviving ghetto life in New York City. Sad, funny, fascinating, and honest in its description of life and death as seen through a child's vision.

Mumford, Lewis, *Green Memories* (New York: Harcourt, Brace and World, 1947).
Geddes, the son of the author, was killed in World War II when he was nineteen. An insight into the heart of a loving and bereaved parent.

Segal, Erich, *Love Story* (New York: Harper and Row, Publishers, 1970).
A sweet, sad, sentimental story of life and death.

Williams, Oscar, ed., *The Pocket Book of Modern Verse* (New York: Washington Square Press, 1958).
Some magnificent poetry dealing with the subject of death: Emily Dickinson's "I Felt a Funeral in My Brain," D. H. Lawrence's "The Ship of Death," John Masefield's "There, on the Darkened Deathbed," Walt Whitman's "When Lilacs Last in the Dooryard Bloom'd," and others.

SUGGESTED BOOKS ABOUT DEATH AND CHILDREN

The following volumes are devoted to the child's perception of life and death.

Anthony, Sylvia, *The Child's Discovery of Death* (New York: Harcourt Brace, 1940).

Ms. Anthony is one of the first to have made a comprehensive study of the subject of children and death based on observations of school children through story completion tests as well as by children's spontaneous talk as kept by their parents. She based her interpretation upon the Freudian principle that to a child death meant little more than departure or disappearance. Her approach is that consciousness of death develops with the intellect rather than on the basis of chronological age.

Cook, Sarah S., ed., *Children and Dying* (New York: Health Sciences Publishing Corporation, 1974).

The book is divided into two sections: how children feel and react to death, and how adults react to the sick, dying, or bereaved child. In a chapter, "The Widow's View of Her Dependent Children," Silverman and Englander write, "Children can misunderstand their mother's silence and think that their mother does not miss their father or care about him."

Fargues, Marie, *The Child and the Mystery of Death* (Glenn Rock, New Jersey: Dews Books, 1966).

Written under the auspices of the Paulists in France, Madame Fargues' book is a lucid blending of modern psychology and Catholic education concerning the child's understanding of the mystery of death. Included are discussion questions for teachers and clergy.

Grollman, Earl A., ed., *Explaining Death to Children* (Boston: Beacon Press, 1967).

A volume by outstanding writers from all of America's major religious faiths plus the fields of anthropology, biology, children's literature, psychiatry, psychology, and sociology. The authors stress that it is not harsh reality that undermines a child's emotional stability but the deprivation of love, understanding, and trust by those adults responsible for the youngster's spiritual, emotional, and physical well-being.

Jackson, Edgar N., *Telling a Child About Death* (New York: Channel Press, 1965).

Dr. Jackson writes with a rare combination of honesty, simplicity, and a profound respect for human dignity in telling a child about death. He covers such questions as when and how to talk about death and what to say to children of different ages.

Mitchell, Marjorie E., *The Child's Attitude to Death* (New York: Schocken Books, 1967).

When a child becomes aware of death, his emotional reactions may be expressed in two simple sentences—"I don't want to die" and "I don't want you to die." The writer attempts to understand children's emotions from religious, scientific, and sociological points of view.

Wolf, Anna M., *Helping Your Child to Understand Death* (New York: Child Study Press, 1973).

A revised edition of this classic brings new material on the effects on the young of mass-media violence, televised war, and upheavals in traditional religious and moral values. As the former senior staff member of the Child Study Association of America, she writes with understanding and compassion.

A RECOMMENDED CASSETTE TAPE SERIES ON DEATH, GRIEF, AND BEREAVEMENT

Center for Death Education and Research
University of Minnesota
1167 Social Science Building
Minneapolis, Minnesota 55455

In the Center's desire to bring recent and relevant ideas concerning the important subject of death to as wide an audience as possible, the following cassette tapes have been made available to the public.

1. "Dialogue on Death"

Dr. John Brantner, Professor of Clinical Psychology, School of Health Sciences, University of Minnesota; Professor Robert Slater, Director, Department of Mortuary Science, University of Minnesota; Dr. Robert Fulton, Professor, Department of Sociology, University of Minnesota and Director, Center for Death Education and Research; Moderator, Connie Goldman, programming staff, KUOM, University of Minnesota Radio. The discussion deals with contemporary American attitudes toward death as well as with such specific issues as the funeral, grief, and mourning.

2. "Stages of Dying"

Dr. Elizabeth Kübler-Ross, Medical Director, Family Service and Mental Health Center of South Cook County, Chicago Heights, Illinois; author of *On Death and Dying*. Dr. Ross tells of her first experience of learning about death from the dying. She describes her theory of the five stages of dying and the symbolic language dying patients often use in an attempt to communicate their feelings.

3. "Death and the Family: From the Caring Professions' Point of View"

Delphie Fredlund, Associate Professor, Public Health Nursing, School of Public Health, University of Minnesota. Professor Fredlund discusses children's attitudes toward death. She underscores the need for children to be made aware of death and for them to learn to accept loss in a realistic and healthy manner.

4. "Social Reconstruction After Death"

Dr. Jeannette Folta, Associate Professor of Psychiatry, University of Vermont, Burlington. Dr. Folta asks the question whether grief is due to the loss of the dead or to the loss sustained by the living.

She comments on the inability of the living to shift social relations and to reintegrate the separate roles the deceased had filled in his lifetime.

5. "The Meaning of Death in American Society"

Dr. Herman Feifel, Clinical Professor of Psychiatry, School of Medicine, University of Southern California, and Chief Psychologist, Veterans Administration. Dr. Feifel offers the general proposition that our society has failed to accept death as a life experience. He discusses the implications of this modern development, both for the individual and for society.

6. "Today's Funeral Director—His Responsibilities and Challenges"

Mr. Glenn Griffin, Griffin-Sparks Funeral Home, Pontiac, Michigan, Past President of the NFDA. Mr. Griffin characterizes the contemporary American funeral as an organized, purposeful, group-centered response to death. He examines the role of the modern funeral director in terms of his actual and potential service to survivors.

7. "A Psycho-Social Aspect of Terminal Care: Anticipatory Grief"

Dr. Robert Fulton, Professor, Department of Sociology, University of Minnesota. Dr. Fulton surveys present-day social and medical practices in America as they affect the chronically ill or dying person. He speculates upon the implications of disengagement from society for the individual as well as for the family and community life.

8. "Death and the Self"

Dr. John Brantner, Professor of Clinical Psychology, School of Health Sciences, University of Minnesota. Dr. Brantner observes that even in the absence of anything that can be called education for death, we do manage, from early childhood on, to learn certain attitudes toward death. It is his premise that we rarely examine or question these attitudes, which today present serious difficulties for many. He descusses necessary changes in such attitudes that will make possible more fully developed lives.

9. "Facing Death with the Patient—An Ongoing Contract"

Dr. Vincent Hunt, Director, Department of Family Practice and Community Health, St. Paul–Ramsey Hospital, St. Paul, Minnesota. Dr. Hunt outlines the general principles he has found effective when dealing with dying patients, and comments on the major areas of concern.

10. "Religious Faith and Death: Implications in Work with the Dying Patient and Family"

The Reverend Carl Nighswonger, Supervisor of Chaplains, University of Chicago Hospital. The Reverend Nighswonger discusses dying as the possible source of a rich, personal, and social experience, particularly if one is allowed to participate in all of its appropriate emotions and feelings. He stresses the need to acknowledge openly to the dying and to their families the fears and emotions associated with a death.

11. "The Role of the Schools in Death Education"

Dr. Daniel Leviton, Professor of Health Education, University of Maryland, College Park, Maryland. Dr. Leviton expresses his views on a need for "formal death education" in the schools. He compares such education to sex education and stresses the value of an academic context. Discussion of the formal classroom situation, teacher and parent education, and the prospect of crisis-intervention facilities are included in Dr. Leviton's talk.

12. "Bereavement and the Process of Mourning"

Dr. Paul Irion, Professor of Pastoral Theology, Lancaster Theological Seminary. Dr. Irion conceptualizes loss in terms of disrupted social relationships. He argues that the social adjustment of a bereaved individual is facilitated by the expression of his authentic feelings. Funerary ritual and other mourning processes provide structured outlets for the ventilation of strong feelings of grief.

13. "The Widow in America: A Study of the Older Widow"

Dr. Helena Lopata, Director, Center for Comparative Study of Social Roles, Loyola University, Chicago. Dr. Lopata explores the psychological and sociological problems created by widowhood in contemporary society. She cites age, education, and socioeconomic status as important factors in the widow's attempt to reenter a society that oftentimes stigmatizes her.

14. "Talking to Children About Death"

Dr. George G. Williams, Associate Professor of Psychology and Public Health, University of Minnesota. Dr. Williams discusses ways to open the channels of communication between parent and child on the sensitive issue of death. He cautions us that thwarting children's efforts at a greater understanding of death can result in serious emotional problems in later life.

15. "Crib Death—The Sudden Infant Death Syndrome. A Documentary"

Dr. John I. Coe, Professor of Pathology, School of Medicine, University of Minnesota, and Carolyn Szybist, R.N., Board Member of the National Foundation for Sudden Infant Death, Inc. Each year 10,000 apparently healthy babies die suddenly and unexpectedly from crib death. Parents who have experienced the loss of a child through SIDS discuss the guilt and self-criticism that exacerbates their normal grief reaction. Dr. Coe presents recent research findings and Ms. Szybist offers suggestions to help parents recover from their loss.

16. "Death and the Child"

Dr. Edgar N. Jackson, psychologist and clergyman, Corinth, Vermont. Dr. Jackson directs his remarks to parents and to those in the caregiving professions who will ultimately shape children's attitudes toward death. Direct, honest answers to their questions on death provide a basis for a healthy philosophy that can sustain an individual throughout life.

17. "Conversation with a Dying Friend"
Connie Goldman, Producer-Reporter, National Public Radio, KSJN, Minneapolis, Minnesota. Ms. Goldman allows us to eavesdrop on a conversation she had with her friend Margie, who is dying of cancer. Margie's very personal account poignantly illuminates the fear and frustration associated with imminent death. She relates to Connie her struggle to grow into the enriched reality of one who has come to terms with her own death.

18. "Adolescent Suicide. A Documentary"
Dr. Norman Farberow, Director, Suicide Prevention Center, Los Angeles. Dr. Farberow and his staff, along with other specialists, discuss the rising incidence of suicide among America's youth and speculate on the reasons. Included are interviews with young men and women who have attempted suicide, a discussion of the impact of suicide on survivors, and some observations on suicide prevention and intervention.

RECOMMENDED FILMS ON DEATH AND DYING

Film and television are the most powerful and pervasive media of our time. The following films are excellent introductions and stimuli for discussions on death and dying. It is suggested that you preview each picture to determine just how it may serve your audience. Determine in advance the questions that the film might raise and the insights you could present. Since there are developmental differences, the filmography is divided into two sections: "For Younger Children" and "For Older Youth."

For Younger Children

The Day Grandpa Died
11 minutes, color. BFA Educational Media, 2211 Michigan Avenue, Santa Monica, California 90404.
When David learns of his grandfather's death, he rushes into the room screaming: "I don't want him dead." The setting is an upper-middle-class Jewish suburban home. There are flashbacks to memories of the happily shared activities of David and his grandfather. For ages 10–15.

Death of a Goldfish
30 minutes, color; program #231 in Mister Rogers' Neighborhood. Family Communications, Inc., 4802 Fifth Avenue, Pittsburgh, Pennsylvania 15213.
A dead fish is found floating on top of the water. Mr. Rogers tries to revive it but in vain. At the conclusion Mr. Rogers says, "It helps to say that you're sad, and if you feel like crying, cry, and if

you feel like running around, then just run around. Each person is different."

In My Memory

14½ minutes, color. Inside/out Series Film, National Instructional Television, Box A, Bloomington, Indiana 47401.

A young girl's response to the death of her grandmother. She cries: "Grandma left me alone; she didn't want to be with me anymore." Especially recommended for third and fourth graders.

Mister Roger's Special: Kennedy Assassination

1 hour, black and white. Family Communications, Inc., 4802 Fifth Avenue, Pittsburgh, Pennsylvania 15213.

A moving, poignant film on the death of Senator Robert Kennedy. Mr. Rogers says, "The best thing in the world is for your children to be included in your family ways of coping with the problems that present themselves. There are those who will find great comfort in being able to sit and watch a television mass of a funeral, so long as it is included in the family. For other families, maybe a walk by a river. . . . For others, maybe just a strong arm around the body of a small child."

My Turtle Died Today

8 minutes, color. BFA Educational Media, 2211 Michigan Avenue, Santa Monica, California, 90404.

Despite the combined efforts of a boy's father, teacher, and a pet-store owner, a sick turtle dies.

Rabbit

15½ minutes, color. Eccentric Circle Cinema Workshop, P.O. Box 1481, Evanston, Illinois 60204.

A good children's film for an introduction to the subject of death. At the outset a boy is faced with a dilemma of how to dispose of a family of rabbits which he has been told he may not keep. His decision on one of the rabbits leads to its death. When he discovers this, the boy is saddened and made to ponder the consequences of his act.

Understanding Death

A sound filmstrip series from
      Educational Perspectives Associates,
      Post Office Box 213
      DeKalb, Illinois 60115.

For the middle school student. Each filmstrip comes with accompanying teacher's guide. Filmstrips are from 50 to 65 frames in length; playing time, 12 to 15 minutes.

    "Explaining the Cemetery"

Burial, memorials, cremation are among the topics covered.

    "Facts About Funerals"

The filmstrip tells of a boy who visits a funeral home and then reports to the class on his findings.

    "A Taste of Blackberries"

Adapted from the book by Doris B. Smith about a young boy's

best friend who dies suddenly (see *Facing the Other Part of Life*).
   "Children and Death"
   How to help children build an understanding of death. A valuable
resource for schools, churches, PTA sessions, and community
organizations by David Berg and George Daugherty.

For Older Youth

All the Way Home
   103 minutes, black and white. Films Incorporated, 1144 Wilmette
Avenue, Wilmette, Illinois 60091.
   Based on James Agee's, *A Death in the Family*, the movie is not
as concerned with the impact of death on a child as the novel was;
still, a good film for older children and adults. Judith Crist writes:
"Sensitivity and subtlety are indeed present and we are engrossed by
time and place and people." For ages 14 and older.

Brian's Song
   75 minutes, color. Learning Corporation of America, 1350 Avenue
of the Americas, New York, New York 10019.
   A true story, dramatized for television, about the professional
football player, Brian Piccolo, and the impact of his death of cancer
at age 26.

A Case of Suicide
   30 minutes, black and white. Time-Life Films, Inc., New York,
New York 10001.
   "I made an appointment with a psychiatrist but she wouldn't
go," Katie's mother says. "She's got a job. I thought she wanted to
work things out for herself. I don't think I can understand why
she killed herself." This British documentary examines the events
that precipitated Katie's suicide and explores the helpless grief
felt by her young widower, her mother, and a friend.

A Conference for the Dying Child
   44 minutes, black and white. Video Nursing, 2834 Central Street,
Evanston, Illinois 60201.
   A nurse's emotions in caring for a dying child. Discusses the
support to be given the patient and family.

The Cry for Help
   33 minutes, black and white. Du Art Film Laboratory, New York,
New York 10019.
   The film suggests ways of handling some of the delicate problems
stemming from suicide attempts. Dramatic episodes about a girl
whose boyfriend didn't call, a middle-aged woman disappointed
in love, a boy who faced an examination, a police officer who
developed heart trouble, and others.

Dead Birds
   81 minutes, black and white. Audio-Visual Center, Indiana
University, Bloomington, Indiana 47401.
   An excellent cross-cultural approach to the life and customs of

the Baliem Valley people of Western New Guinea. The film explores their death customs as well as other tribal traditions.

Death

42 minutes, black and white. University of California, Extension Media Center, 2223 Fulton Street, Berkeley, California 94720.

A documentary which reveals how poorly prepared most people are for the terror and isolation of dying. The film follows a 52-year-old terminal cancer patient through his last days in a city hospital. Physicians discuss the psychology of dying and defenses of the dying person.

Diary of Anne Frank

150 minutes, color. Films Incorporated, 1144 Wilmette Avenue, Wilmette, Illinois 60091.

Based on the classic autobiography of Anne Frank (see *Facing the Other Part of Life*), this is a portrayal of her adolescent years in the secret attic hideout in Amsterdam in World War II. Bosley Crowther of the *New York Times* wrote, ". . . The magnificence of human endurance and compassion . . . shines in virtually every character."

Explaining Death to Children

60 minutes, black and white. Shands Teaching Hospital, University of Florida, Gainesville, Florida 32601.

A videotape of Earl A. Grollman's discussion on death and children at the University of Florida, with questions from the college students.

Forbidden Games

90 minutes, black and white. Janus Films, 745 Fifth Avenue, New York, New York 10022.

A little girl is orphaned by Nazi strafing of a column of fleeing refugees that included her family. Amid the chaos of war she and a little boy with whose family she comes to live build a "play cemetery" in which they bury dead animals dragged from the battle-fields. In French, with English subtitles, the film is for ages 14 and older.

Gift of Life/Right to Die

15 minutes, black and white. University of California, Extension Media Center, 2223 Fulton Street, Berkeley, California 94720.

What happens when a patient is dying and another sorely needs one of his organs for transplantation? Physicians cite ideas on euthanasia as well as discussions on medical ethics and other controversial situations.

How Could I Not Be Among You?

29 minutes, color. Eccentric Circle Cinema Workshop, P.O. Box 1481, Evanston, Illinois 60204.

Portrait of a poet who is about to die and knows it. Ted Rosenthal had leukemia and had about six months to live. Filmed during his last months, the picture captures the agony and hope of a gifted young man. For ages 16 and up this film has been widely hailed by medical and education professionals.

I Never Sang For My Father

92 minutes, color. Macmillan Audio Brandon, 34 MacQuesten Parkway, South, Mt. Vernon, New York 10550.

The death of a wife leaves a tyrannical older man in conflict with his middle-aged son. Death causes various identity problems.

The Last Full Measure of Devotion

27½ minutes, color. National Funeral Directors Association, 135 West Wells Street, Milwaukee, Wisconsin 53203.

The highlights of the John F. Kennedy funeral and the emotional impact of his death as compared with the ceremonies for Lincoln and Franklin Roosevelt. How a nation cares for its dead leaders.

Love Story

100 minutes, color. Films Incorporated, 1144 Wilmette Avenue, Wilmette, Illinois 60091.

Film production of Erich Segal's bittersweet novel (see *Facing the Other Part of Life*) about the love of Oliver Barrett IV and Jenny Cavilleri. Jenny dies at age 25 and Oliver and his estranged father become reconciled.

An Occurrence at Owl-Creek Bridge

28 minutes, black and white. Visual Aids Service, University of Illinois, Division of University Extension, Champaign, Illinois 61822.

The dramatization of Ambrose Bierce's short story about an incident in the Civil War. A young Southerner about to be hanged for sabotage manages to escape when the rope breaks. Death, however, is not an abstraction but a reality as he contemplates the real meaning of life. For ages 14 and up.

Perspectives on Death

A sound filmstrip series from
> Educational Perspectives Associates
> Post Office Box 213
> DeKalb, Illinois 60115

For the high school student, the program consists of four components: an audio-visual package containing two color-sound films and two separate tape-cassette presentations, an anthology of readings, a student activity book, and a teacher's resource book. The audio-visual package includes the following:

"Funeral Customs Around the World."
> A 110-frame color filmstrip with cassette narration, exploring funeral customs around the world.

"Death Through the Eyes of the Artist"
> How the artist has attempted through style, color, subject matter, and symbolism to capture the mood of death.

"Death Themes in Literature"
> Authors, poets, and dramatists bring their literary insights into understanding death.

"Death Themes in Music"
    Musicians express their emotions through classical, jazz, folk, and modern music.

Designed as a six-week mini-course or to be incorporated within the existing English or social studies program.

The Right to Live: Who Decides
    17 minutes, black and white. Learning Corporation of America, 1350 Avenue of the Americas, New York, New York, 10019.
    A captain decides to sacrifice some lives in order to save others.

Sunrise Semester Segment
    28½ minutes, color. National Funeral Directors Association, 135 West Wells Street, Milwaukee, Wisconsin 53203.
    A dialogue between Dr. James A. Carse of New York University, and Mr. Howard C. Raether, Executive Director of NFDA, viewing many phases of the funeral and the conflicts as to rites and ceremonies following death.

Too Personal to Be Private
    27½ minutes, color. National Funeral Directors Association, 135 West Wells Street, Milwaukee, Wisconsin 53203.
    A highly useful film, which portrays what the funeral has been, what it is, and what it can do. Describes some of the reactions and responses of a family to the emotional crisis of death.

When Parents Grow Old
    15 minutes, color. Learning Corporation of America, 1350 Avenue of the Americas, New York, New York, 10019. For junior and senior high school students as well as college students.
    Faced with the problems of a suddenly widowed father whose health is failing, a young man on the verge of marriage must decide where his responsibilities lie. The theme is the problem of responsibility to aging parents and society's treatment of the elderly.

Widows
    43 minutes, black and white. Mental Health Training Film Program, Harvard Medical School, 33 Fenwood Road, Boston, Massachusetts 02115.
    Widows discuss the deaths of their husbands, their grief, and the kinds of help they found useful.

You See, I've Had a Life
    32 minutes, black and white. Eccentric Circle Cinema Workshop, P.O. Box 1481, Evanston, Illinois 60204.
    A thirteen-year-old boy is stricken with leukemia. As the story unfolds, each hospital visit leaves him closer to his untimely death. Fortunately, he has a family who, rather than hide the illness from him, shares the final meaningful experiences of death. For ages 14 and older—senior high or college, and adult groups and mental health associations.